UNDERSTANDING
THE ENGLISH

by

JAMES HOWARD WELLARD

New York WHITTLESEY HOUSE *London*

MCGRAW-HILL BOOK COMPANY, INC.

914.2
W48

PUBLISHED BY WHITTLESEY HOUSE
A division of the McGraw-Hill Book Company, Inc.

Printed in the United States of America by The Maple Press Co., York, Pa.

Preface

IT WAS not until the author had lived for a time outside his own country that he became aware of the
incredulity felt by other peoples toward his compatriots. Abroad, there was no avoiding the suspicion
that the English do look, from a distance, mysterious
and non-human. These notions have been expressed,
sometimes with wit and gusto, sometimes with pain
and astonishment, by numerous foreign critics; and
the gist of the matter has been well summed up by an
Italian journalist, one Curzio Malaparte, who advances
the attractive thesis that the English are not of this
world at all.

Informal acknowledgments, then, are due those
foreign observers whose delightful attempts at mis-
understanding the English suggested to the present
writer that readers might like an attempt to understand his people by way of a contrast.

Formal acknowledgments are made to those publications in which some of the author's ideas and conclusions
on the subject of the English were first put forward.
Among these publications is the *Yale Review* in the
Winter, 1937, number of which first appeared an essay
by this author entitled "On Understanding the English."
Special thanks are tendered to the editors of the *Yale
Review* for their kindness in readily giving permission
to reproduce or adapt the material of this article.

v

Appreciation is also expressed to the *Nineteenth Century and After* for permission to use again material first published in an article "Observations on American Prose"; to the *Quarterly Review* for an article "English and the Need of an Academy," published in the July, 1930, number of that journal; and to *The International Quarterly* for an article "English Class Distinctions," published in January, 1937.

Possibly some gratitude should be recorded to the subjects of this study in consideration of their patience under the microscope.

JAMES HOWARD WELLARD.

CHICAGO, ILLINOIS.

Contents

Book III
LIFE

UNDERSTANDING
THE ENGLISH

INTRODUCTION

England

Atlantic Landfall

THE American first sees England a distant coast on the horizon. It seems fitting to him that he should see it so. There is no sign of habitation, no demonstrative welcome, such as his own country affords him with the glimpse of a city seen long before the smell of land reaches his nostrils. For a time England is just a dark island, and the traveler approaches it with much the same tense expectancy that the Phoenicians felt off the Cornish Coast three thousand years earlier. England, from the Atlantic, is an enchanted island.

As the liners near the coast, the independent life on shipboard abruptly ends and has no more meaning. Delightful friendships are tacitly forgotten; meals, deck sports, confidences in the saloon, and the contentment of afternoons by the rail are all broken. Ship life suddenly seems tedious, and the overwhelming impatience of the explorer seizes the passenger gazing landward. What is over the rim of those smooth, green hills and what new cove is hidden behind the next headland?

Curiosity is partly satisfied and partly stimulated by a nearer view of the land. One realizes with a faint

3

shock that wonder is giving way to facts. Green grass, woods, roads, and horses are at once a source of gratification and disillusionment. Small towns spread around the bays with that finality the American expects of history. They are as much a part of the landscape as the bouncing coasters which wallow to leeward are part of the sea. It is fitting that the houses are low and built of warm brick. It is fitting that they have red roofs and that one long factory chimney rises smokeless on the outskirts of the town. Thus England must always have looked to the foreign sailor, an expected surprise in which all his anticipations are gradually materialized.

Not even in the harbor is there disappointment. A tender arrives from nowhere, as it should. It carries a load of strangely silent stevedores, unofficious officials with the minimum of gold braid, and a newsboy with the inevitable London *Times*. The captain of the tender stands square on the bridge, with his hand on the telegraph. The mate stands in the bows. They are manifestly born seamen—manifestly, from their wide-legged stance, from their silence, from the way their great coats are turned up at the collar. So with the sailor, brewing tea in the galley. They would navigate ships, one feels, over the rim of the earth, hunched on the bridge, expectant in the bows, and brewing tea in the galley.

There is no need, of course, to feel any reverence or violent emotion on stepping ashore. A tightening of the throat is enough. The quiet mood of three hours previous is lost in wonder and amusement. The toy freight cars, the squeak of a distant engine, the stolidity of the tin advertisements nailed to walls, the fantastic language which is being spoken, and the preposterous re-

4

spectability of the English money, stimulate an inward glow of mirth. Everything is just as it should be. The harbor inn is called "Fisherman's Rest" and announces "Courage's Fine Beers. Ale and Stout." Inside, the circular counter is of scrubbed wood. The beer engines are black, neatly circled with brass rings and pulled by bouncing barmaids. Fishermen in blue jerseys stand with pint glasses in front of them. A coal fire burns in the grate. A dog nibbles his fleas.

The boat train quietly illustrates that most characteristic of English attitudes—class distinctions. There are first- and third-class compartments, and it is difficult to see any difference in them as far as cleanliness and comfort are concerned. The compartments, too, imply certain concessions to the English passion for privacy: six people and no more to a carriage, and when the carriage is full one slides a door and shuts out the rest of the world, then in silence travels Londonward.

This first sight of England from a railway carriage window, whether one travels up from Plymouth or Newhaven, is a confirmation to all foreigners of their preconceptions about this strange island. Those who expect a green and luscious landscape see such slide by them, with many a detail they had overlooked: a solitary ploughman with his dappled horse, for instance, a man indifferent to time and circumstances. He is a symbol of a race, and his resemblance to his Saxon ancestors is apparent in the furrow he traces in the downland. Those who look for lanes and hedged roads find lanes and more; there are brick bridges and level crossings at every railway station, with flocks of cyclists waiting. A thousand years of uninterrupted history is there: cottages, castles, cathedral spires, and red brick towns with names as fabulous as Troy. The traveler is delighted. Horses look over hedges, cows doze on the grass, children wave from the fields—magnificent horses, charming children; but where are the English, and who are they?

As the foreigner nears London, he sees the green country give way to cricket fields and park land. Rows of identically hideous villas suddenly blot out the country. Villas change into houses, houses into tenements, tenements into factories. The air grows darker. Not even a name like "Vauxhall" can romanticize a station full of milk churns. The ominous might of London oppresses the stranger. There is no longer a sensation of expectancy to enliven or the charm of rusticity to soothe him. He suddenly feels intimidated. The train which was small and cheerful at Plymouth Harbor, has become large and relentless at King's Cross. There is no more an inward mirth at a miniature world. King's Cross is a huge cavern, full of the thunder of wheels and the hiss of steam. Escaping, one looks through the taxi window at London and for the first time sees the English people. One's spirits rise. These people not only look pleasant, they actually look human. A bus goes by with the conductor hanging by a crooked arm to the brass rail on the platform. A brewer's dray is driven by a character right out of Dickens. A telegraph boy in a pillbox cap whistles loudly. And statuesque at the crossing, embodying the law and the spirit of England, stands a London bobby—a proof, in his Roman helmet, that England is unshaken by the hurry and changes and catastrophes which rock the rest of the world.

6

Book I

P E O P L E

I

Who Are the English?

FOR over a century now, the English have had the reputation among foreigners of not belonging to the human race. According to certain observers, they are segregated from other men even in heaven. This was the contention of Swedenborg, for instance. Other critics, while not so sure of the place of the English in the next world, are quite certain that they do not belong in this. They are here on earth entirely by accident. Indeed, so bright are their countenances (says a recent Italian), so blond is their hair, so melodious are their voices, that none could account them earthly beings of flesh and bone. They must, he continues, have alighted from a cloud. Their ways and looks are not of this world.

This cherubic conception of the English, however, is not by any means general. While there undoubtedly is a well-defined pink type of Englishman, fresh from the University and all nicely groomed for a foreign consulate, pinkness would not be universally accepted as the dominant color of the Anglo-Saxons. The French, to the contrary, are irritated by the grayness of the English: by their gray clothes, gray expressions, gray climate, and gray food. The Romans, in their time, found the English, like true barbarians, had painted themselves blue. Minor European nations endow them with the complexion of their favorite wine, port. The Chinese consider them green. And to most Americans the average Englishman would be parti-colored—in character as in costume—a sort of brown at the top and gray below. But whatever their color, there is no doubt among the peoples of the rest of the world that the English are not human. They neither do what other men do nor apparently feel what other men feel. Together with mad dogs, they run out into the midday sun. Like the camels, they have countenances expressing no emotions. And like the yak, they maintain a vast silence, which can only be the cloak of wisdom.

In spite of all these unhuman traits, and probably because of them, the English are yielded a begrudged but definite homage, in the form either of irritation or of envy. Even the French, so indifferent to the rest of the world, pay tribute to the English in concessions of fear and respect. The Germans are mute with admiration, the Italians desperate with envy, to the extent of adopting English customs and fashions of a decade or so ago. Wherever in Europe, for that matter, one sees an honest citizen whose thick neck is constricted by a white collar, whose lumpy head carries a hard round hat, whose hairy legs are tightly encased in striped trousers and whose strong, short hands are covered by violent yellow gloves, there one is seeing an individual tribute to the English. These same clothes, as the whole world knows, *they* can wear with grace and comfort, for their necks are thin, their heads finely oval, their legs long, and their hands delicate, so that their bodies demand to be encased in a costume whose formality suppresses every suggestion of warmth and humanity.

If there was ever a negation of life and movement and color, it must be a British cabinet minister arriving for a conference at Number 10 Downing Street. Slightly stooping, the minister alights from his taxi, no more vivid or exciting than the folded umbrella he invariably carries as the challenge of good form to the elements. It must be because the English are not human that they can wear clothes with the precision of a tailor's dummy, and the rest of the world is driven by some indefinable attraction to imitate them.

In Scandinavia tight black trousers split as the good burgher sits down to dinner. In Turkey some Mustapha apes the apes in a funeral top hat. In the Belgian Congo the native chieftain regards a rusty "bowler" as the most impressive part of his trappings. And in Sierra Leone the hefty porter runs through the streets in an old Bond Street necktie. One feels, somehow, that these English garments sit oddly on Scandinavian burgher and African cannibal alike. These men are too human. Their faces light up or are darkened. Their voices are heard expressing their feelings or opinions without shame. They laugh and rumble and perspire and surreptitiously eructate. The English, apparently, do none of these things; they are, in comparison, celestial.

The Americans are seemingly not intimidated by even the nonterrestrial quality of the English; the frigidity which awes the European, the accent which so effectively puts lesser breeds in their place, the scrupulous courtesy which terrifies ordinary mortals are all explained away by a special brand of American cynicism: the English can't help it; it's just their bad luck that they are that way. Their frigidity is passed off as snootiness; their accent, according to H. L. Mencken,[1] as suspicious, like male tea drinking, spats, and wrist watches; their unflinching politeness, as a lack of humor. Mind you, there is nonetheless considerable awe on the part of the Americans in the presence of a people who keep a monarch in his place, rule one-third of the world, and retain so many remarkable, if somewhat useless, customs and relics. Not even American cynicism can dispel a feeling of reverence in the presence of Culture; the influence of their women is felt too strongly in this respect.

English visitors have for generations been getting away with all manner of saucy criticisms of the American people, which this usually assertive race accepts in a strangely humble fashion. It is like the spectacle of the big, strong man being told off by a little, squeaky one. Moreover, such treatment would not be tolerated from anyone else. A Chinaman could not inform the Americans that they are noisy, materialistic, and over-partial to expectorating. The roars of the American Legion would rise high in accusations of subversive propaganda. Only the women's clubs would tolerate such criticism, and they would tolerate anything during

---

[1] MENCKEN, H. L., *The American Language*, Alfred A. Knopf, Inc., New York, 1919.

the weekly hour set aside for Culture. In his way, then, the irrepressible American is abashed in the face of the unhumanity of the English. For not even he can get to the bottom of this strange creature or exorcise him with one of those twinkling sallies which have successfully debunked most other pretensions.

In America, as everywhere else, the English are so very English, remote, mysterious, and unhuman. They carry their supposed secret into the small towns of North Dakota and New Mexico. Everywhere they have that national ability of making men feel uncomfortable, a trifle envious, and guiltily human. Few can penetrate their masks or their minds. Almost everyone gives up the attempt, assuming that the English defy analysis and explaining this assumption by supposing them a breed apart—superhuman, if you like, but by no stretch of the imagination human. From Julius Caesar to André Maurois, says the foreign critic, none has ever succeeded in telling us what the English are or in giving us the clue that would enable us to penetrate their secret. This is true; it is all the more true, because there is no secret. There are only facts and customs and modes of behavior. Knowledge of these things does not make the Englishman, any more than an analysis of the parts of a living cell make the synthesis known as life; but it helps us to understand and brings what is otherwise a mystery into the scope of human comprehension. So, too, the English can be analyzed and fitted into their place in the universe—not only into the universe, but into the human race, to which, in spite of their appearance and behavior, even the most skeptical must admit they belong.

2

In these large times of compulsory education and reader's digests, most foreigners have a rough idea where the land of the English is and some knowledge of what it looks like. Especially Americans' knowledge of the country is increasing. It is known, for instance, that the majority of the English now bathe once a week, as contrasted to the German monthly dip and the French biannual scrub. The English, as it were, are now only six days behind the Americans, and are catching up fast. They are hastening to speak the American language and to adapt their mode of life to the American way. There is no longer the same strong moral opposition to the innumerable little conveniences, such as vacuum cleaners, safety razors, central heating, iced water, and chewing gum, which might be considered America's contribution to the amenities of existence.

The English are learning rapidly how to live in automobiles and how to sustain themselves on canned foods. Some of the men actually have their clothes cleaned and pressed, and the women are dressing more to please than to forbid, as of old. The latter still retain the individual and stern dowdiness from the knees down, and have refused so far to make their feet look anything but large and flat. But their drawers, even though as voluminous and prim as formerly, are no longer an additional protection to the navel and ankles. Since one of Shakespeare's queens cried with all the pathos one would expect of an Englishwoman in the circumstances, "What stays had I but they, and they are gone!" the absence of corsets has been considered condoned by royalty, with very beneficial and pretty results to the English figure.

The country of England lies, together with Labrador, Alaska, and Siberia, above latitude 50, a position which may have some significance in view of the characteristic English frigidity. As a matter of fact, it is never particularly cold in these parts, thanks to the only central heating system America has been able to introduce into the Islands, namely, the Gulf Stream. If it were cold in England, instead of merely damp and wet, the English would have had worse complexions but less rheumatism. The dreariness of the weather, in brief, like the prevalence of red noses throughout the long winter fogs, has helped mold the English character or, rather, the national point of view. For the English are the only people who moralize physical discomfort. Their greatest moral achievements have been typified by a fierce ingenuity in the art of being uncomfortable.

The Victorian home was such a moral masterpiece. The houses were built as though with the express purpose of wearing out the housewife with labor, while making sure of killing off the servant by confining her activities to the basement. In order that none of the family should relax, chairs were made high and straight, and expressly stuffed with horsehair in order to prick the backs of small boys' legs, as a reproof, evidently, of any display of cheerfulness. One room, especially, was kept with a view to impressing the outside world with the coldness and discomfort of home—the parlor, an invariably fireless room to which the family retired on Sundays to suffer indigestion in the most dismal surroundings possible. There stood the upright piano, upon which were played the hymns compiled by those masters of dolor, Messrs. Moody and Sankey. For pictures the parlor had the portraits of the immediate ancestors and photographs of father and mother on their wedding day, in which the expressions of the cynically termed "happy couple" eloquently delineated their foreknowledge of doom. For flowers a mottled aspidistra was substituted; for books, a popular science series and the biographies of the more successful tradesmen. In this room, from which all fresh air and sunlight had been excluded for many years, only the aspidistra could flourish. The family grew colder and whiter and unhappier until it was time for bed.

Yet this triumph of uncomfortable living and no thinking, which is the Presbyterian idea of virtue, was not always typical of English life. We have to remember that the English were not always successful and righteous and unhuman. It appears that they were regarded as human by the rest of the world until about the middle of the nineteenth century, when the full significance of the English destiny was proclaimed by the politicans, exploited by the merchants, hymned by the poets, and systematized by the clergy.

In the Middle Ages there was nothing extraordinary in being born an Englishman. An individual like Roger Bacon referred to himself as a Latin, by which he meant a European, one with the European outlook and speaking the European language—a language surviving for us in those hearty drinking songs which still sound magnificently bucolic when roared out after midnight.

The French conviction that the English are fundamentally barbarians was current from about the twelfth century onward. The English were goddamers, roisterers, and surreptitious cannibals. In the polished seventeenth and eighteenth centuries, for that matter, they roared rather than spoke, and snarled their way, in the manner of Tobias Smollett, across the alarmed continent. The French critic, Taine, points out in the literature of Fielding this fundamentally barbarous character of the English. Their idea of fun, in life as in literature, was to pitch a pail of pig's blood over an opponent in an argument over a Latin tag. The ideal English squire was a match for any Turk or Tartar. He could outroar him, to begin with, or eat more or drink more old port and could get redder in the face before bursting a blood vessel.

A glance at the old Norse and Anglo-Saxon sagas will indicate the heredity here; for the English ancestors had never been happier than when killing. As Emerson neatly remarks: they have a singular turn for homicide. If there is no legitimate weapon to hand for the purpose, they seize oars, scythes, harpoons, crowbars, hayforks, or quart tankards. The sight of a tent cord, says Emerson of these Norsemen, puts them in mind of hanging someone, a wife or a husband, and preferably a king. They differ from a southern lynching mob only in that they made a fairly clean job of murder, and did it from a surfeit of roast beef rather than from any ill will.

No one would deny, I take it, that all of this is very human and therefore excusable. No one need take umbrage at a little exuberance and an occasional good time, even if it is of a rather rough variety. After all, mammoths no doubt killed and mated and played in a very different manner from domestic animals. Likewise our conduct today differs largely in degree rather than in kind from that of our ancestors. It is all quite human and understandable. It doesn't puzzle or even shock us. If it does, we should bear in mind how a band of Norsemen would run squealing to their boats before the rat-a-tat of a machine gun, much as a herd of wild horses would thunder off if snapped at by a wire-haired terrier. They would not at all consider the machine gunner a civilized gentleman and would have some justification in asserting the decline of good manners.

What happened to the English, then, to bring about this astonishing change from roisterers with clubs to shopkeepers with umbrellas; from bellowing warriors to taciturn diplomats; from five-bottle men to afternoon tea drinkers? What happened, in other words, to drain them of their recognizable human qualities, only different from their fellows in their native uncouthness, so that today they no longer look, act, or feel like other men? It is a very remarkable fact; so remarkable, indeed, that foreign observers have predicated a mystery to explain it away. The English, they say, have a secret. Fifty million Englishmen with a secret. If the inquirer begins with this premise he will never find a solution to the problem, an answer to the question. Let us not suppose a secret at all. Let us suppose nothing until we have taken the Englishman apart to see whether he is an automaton, manipulated by some unseen director, or simply a human being, caught in the intricacies of his own limitations.

II

The Imaginary Englishman

EVERY people adopts a convenient prototype of the others. This is all right so long as the concept is limited to the music hall and is not made the basis for a nation's foreign policy. We might add, with due sententiousness, that in the latter case we very soon work up a hostile psychology. When the Englishman calls a Frenchman a froggy, he is all ready to fight him; or when the American calls the Englishman a limey, he is itching to sock him on the snoot. Similarly, the advantage of calling a Chinese a Chink or a Japanese a Jap is to inculcate the frame of mind necessary to treat these people with injustice or disdain. The abusive or sneering designations abound—nigger, yid, dago, hun, square-head, and so forth; and in keeping with these symbols, a generalized type is conjured up and invested with all the bad qualities of his race. The predilection of people today for these large, generalized abstractions should be very gratifying to the Greek philosophers, who had a hard time turning young men's thoughts from real

19

beds to the idea of a bed. Nowadays, we have adopted a presumably philosophical approach as far as our knowledge of other men is concerned. FRANCE THREATENS SPAIN, announce the headlines; and soon, MADRID REPLIES. Not only the idea of a thing here, but the idea of an idea. Philosophy happily mated with Journalism; Plato arm in arm with Hearst.

So, in the case of the English we arrive at the imaginary Englishman, the bemonocled aristocrat, the "I say old chappie, dewnt you knaow" individual who is heard bleating from the stage or is seen drifting across the screen. If the films went impressionistic, a monocle would symbolize Sir Niles Travers, the English prototype, as a pair of ears might symbolize Clark Gable and a row of eyelashes Greta Garbo. The monocle would do for "Sir Travers," but some other symbol would have to be found for Simpson, prototype of the butler, perpetuated for all time in the magnificent parody which is Laughton's *Ruggles.* Possibly a pair of striped trousers would do or a voice off stage respectfully murmuring, "Yes, sir. Certainly, sir."

We should note that the popular imagination makes allowance for two types of Englishman, the aristocrat and the servant, whereas there is only one Frenchman, one German, one Russian. Indeed, come to think of it, there is only one personification each, for the Latin, the Teutonic, and the Oriental races: the pointed beard, the cropped head, and the pigtail, respectively. It is interesting that public discernment in America distinguishes between master and servant in the case of the English, thus making allowance for class distinction, that most significant characteristic of English society.

The imaginary Englishman, then. There is John Bull, the florid, rotund farmer, totally unlike any known Englishman, with the possible exception of the Rt. Hon. Stanley Baldwin. A useful concept, though, for political cartoonists, who cling to the outmoded generalizations of eighteenth century polemics—Marianne with some droll pretensions to sex appeal; Uncle Sam, based apparently on a quack medicine vendor operating south of the Mason and Dixon's Line; and John Bull, eighteenth century squire—useful concepts, saving both the ingenuity of the cartoonist and the imagination of the reader. No one, therefore, regards political cartoons based on personifications of national types as anything but ponderous attempts at humor. They have no particular significance, unless one excepts the symbolization of the two leading American parties as two of the less prepossessing animals. But the kind of cartoon in which Uncle Sam with his small ship dolefully proclaims, as the larger English and French liners sail into port, "Well, if they paid me my debts, maybe I could have a big ship too!" generally portrays a sense of humor and a quality of draftsmanship, commonly considered the prerogative of *Punch*.

John Bull is a legendary Englishman, although what could replace him as a personification of Great Britain, it would be puzzling to say. One wonders sometimes if the funereal appearance of such figures as the Rt. Hon. Neville Chamberlain, that diplomatic undertaker, might not be appropriate as representing the traditional British foreign policy based on a combination of Machiavelli and John Wesley. For a period Captain Anthony Eden made an ironically decorative figure in political cartoons, and there was a time when the Rt. Hon. Ramsay Mac-Donald in a maid's costume and handle-bar moustaches symbolized some political pother or other very well indeed. Now there is no significant figure, unless it be Strube's "Little Man" or Low's "Colonel Blimp," the former well typifying with his precarious spectacles and bewildered expression the lower-middle-class Englishman; and the latter immortalizing the retired hero who saved the Empire at Poona and is now saving it from the Army and Navy Club in Pall Mall.

As mythical as the cartoonists' John Bull is the music halls' Archibald Boom-Punkington, groomed by Hollywood into Sir Niles Travers. Archibald Boom-Punkington, though a myth, was a significant type, significant to the extent of having molded the average American opinion of the Englishman, whence the English voice excites far more amusement and derision than its possible resemblance to the distant bleating of a mountain goat really justifies. The provincial American still associates with those refined and emasculated tones the figure of Archibald Boom-Parkington, that willowy, drooping gentleman who goes "Haw! Haw! I say, old top, isn't that good! By Jove, you know, that's jolly funny, what!" ten minutes after the joke has been told. Evidently it doesn't occur to the American that the frosty silence and the mask of boredom with which the Englishman greets one of those after-dinner stories passing for humor in America may be due either to having read the story in a dentist's copy of the *Saturday Evening Post* or, more likely, to having seen the point ten minutes before the raconteur arrived at it. Nonetheless, the provincial clings to his concept of the typical Englishman as a "sorter sissy" with a phony accent, an individual whose mannerisms arouse his social suspicion and whose habit of stuffing a handkerchief in his coat cuff almost furnishes grounds for police interference.

Hollywood, in its strange attempts now at sophistication, now at culture, has metamorphosed this pristine Englishman into the personage of Mr. Leslie Howard, who is not, after all, so very different from Archibald Boom-Punkington. Leslie Howard is all right, of course, and American girls in their eagerness for new sensations became enthusiastic over the idea of a lover who could stroke their hair with such white hands, in contrast to the methods of Dave Bonski (1938); a lover who could murmur, "Your wish, Madame, is my privilege," as compared to the boy last night who was concerned only with the privilege. Nevertheless, to American men and even, in the last analysis, to American women, Leslie Howard is a bit of a sissy. White hands, a fragile profile, expressive eyes, and a cultivated manner are not American attributes. They're just not manly, and a fellow who possesses them may be decorative, but he's not a hundred percenter. Clark Gable comes as a necessary reagent, as a normalizing personification; and when Americans see his large ears and hear his homely voice, they can relax again. The "gentleman" has been exorcized. Yet he, like the other two-dimensional personifications, is but a myth, possible only in a world of Scarlet Pimpernels and Romeos. He is not a real Englishman, and foreigners who base their judgment of the

English on Leslie Howard or Boom-Punkington or "Sir Travers," will never understand them. They will have only a romantic apprehension, and will talk of undiscoverable secrets in order to explain away a hallucination.

Simpson, the butler, contributes in his way to the English myth and the romantic view. Just as Sir Niles Travers represents the legendary English aristocracy, so Simpson offsets the upper class and personifies the lower. He symbolizes respect. He knows his place—knows it so well that Americans, struggling to introduce snobbishness into an inveterately democratic society, regard the English butler as a proof of the superiority of the English system. How charming when Simpson brings in Lord Rathbone's morning cup of tea, while his Lordship moans, "Go away, Simpson. I can't bear you"; and Simpson murmurs, "Yes, your Lordship. But, this is your tea, your Lordship"; and Rathbone with groans no more convincing than his inebriation of the night before, says, "Simpson, you're a positive menace; but indispensable, indispensable." Delightful relationship. Grace on the one side and respect on the other; sparkling conversation (such as the above) on the part of the master, respectful monosyllables from the man. An ideal arrangement. Ideal and idealistic, for the English stage butler is as legendary now as Old King Cole, and has not appeared in any respectable play since *Lady Windermere's Fan*. He is not a significant English type, so that overconcern with him, as with Sir Niles Travers, will not help toward understanding the English. When his portly figure appears like a procession of one on the stage or screen, the audience should put themselves in the frame of mind assumed for other historical travesties, such as Henry the Eighth and Squire Hawkins and Bully Bottom.

2. THE SEMIMYTHICAL ENGLISHMAN

"Blond and pink," says Curzio Malaparte, "the English disembark at Calais as though alighting from a cloud. They leave the deck of the steamer and set foot on shore with a heavenly smile, such as may have lit the faces of the first aeronauts descending from the gondola of their fire balloon. Something of a higher, far-off sphere still lingers about them."

Malaparte, of course, has never seen an Englishman in his life. He has lived in England, studied the English, talked and eaten with them, played and possibly fallen in love with some of them. But he never saw or knew a single specimen. He saw a mythical race, a people of visions, two-dimensional like characters in a film. He was baffled, envious, irritated; and satisfied his curiosity by ascribing his emotions to the English and their "impenetrable secret." Like generations of foreigners, he analyzed his subjects with admirable ingenuity. Avoiding the error of pedantry, he discards facts and figures and any evidence smacking of impartiality; then, assuming what he sets out to prove, he demonstrates with grace and skill that the English are not of this world; that they are, in a word, unhuman. Everybody reads, agrees, and smiles with satisfaction. Meanwhile, fifty million Englishmen trudge about their business on large and unimaginative feet with the unshakable conviction that they are the only ones who matter, after all.

It is indicative of Malaparte's delusion that he considers the English not only blond and pink, but handsome, "with a cold, haughty beauty." This semimyth of English handsomeness seems to be the result of repetition rather than of observation. "Not Angles, but angels," said Gregorius (according to the English historians), and his weak pun has become an unshakable principle. But it is well to remember that his remark applied to the Saxons, before Danes and Normans had added dark complexions and round heads to the English racial physiognomy. Foreign observers care nothing for this, provided they can maintain their point about the unhumanity of the English. This necessitates the "cold, haughty beauty," "the long, white hands," and the frigid expression of the Englishman abroad.

The trouble with European critics is that they have never got over Lord Byron. To the Latin brand of romanticism Byron was the apotheosis of beauty and life: he was handsome—and handsome in that large manner which runs to Greek profiles, black capes, and riding boots; he was a lover—with that ability for the rapid conquest of chambermaids which is the Latin ideal of fornication; and he was a poet—a rhymester, instead of a metaphysician like so many of the English poets. While the average European has not read a word of Byron, he supposes that this poetry is the only English literature which is human enough to praise the pleasures of venery. He concludes, moreover, though more on the ground of hearsay than from any knowledge, that Byron practiced what he preached, suffered a romantic exile, and died the death of a hero.

What more could be asked of any man? And this from an Englishman.

Byron, then, personifies that semimythical type, the romantic young lord who visited the continent in the seventeenth and eighteenth centuries, for no other purpose, according to parents at home, than that of sowing wild oats. Many of these young men were talented dilettantes, with a taste for the more exquisite pleasures. They combined a remarkable soundness of constitution with a peculiar protestant melancholy, which left them sober when other men were drunk, sad when everyone else was gay. This made them both impressive and irritating in the eyes of Europeans. They were like guests who could not be amused, yet compelled attention. They caste a spell wherever they went—and they drifted all over the world, returning home at last to write Gothic novels about Spain or translate Horace into English.

Any foreign observer, therefore, who takes his types from books will accept this formula of the semimythical Englishman. It is droll when one thinks of all those real Englishmen who can be seen by any observer not hypnotized by the certainty of a secret. One thinks of the twenty million workers, most of them gulping beer and playing darts in the four-ale bar of the local pub on a Saturday night. These Englishmen are unknown to foreigners, who could learn more from an evening in the *Yacht* at Greenwich than they could in a year at the Strand Palace Hotel. It is an extraordinary thing that no foreign writer on the English has made allowance in his observations for these twenty million ordinary human beings. They are either lumped together as some proletarian monster or dismissed with a caricatured portrait and a Cockney accent. The foreigner supposes that the English workingman comes somewhere below Simpson, the butler, in the social scale. He is the offspring, as it were, of Simpson and Mrs. 'Awkins, the charwoman, deriving expected characteristics from each.

However, in the large, semimythical generalization of the Englishman, there is no attempt to differentiate class from class. For one thing, the English class system is so complicated that no foreigner, and above all, no American, can be expected to understand it. For an American there are apparently "dooks," sirs, and others. He would not know what to make of the first if he ever met one, for a duke would strike him as such a freak that he would be dumb from wonder rather than awe. "Sirs," having on occasions sold their birthright to Hollywood for a small part in a film or having put themselves on exhibition on lecture platforms for sums a gas-station attendant would consider modest, are no longer causes for any particular wonder; so that it is increasingly difficult for Americans to evaluate the significance of class in England. To the less sophisticated all Englishmen have class by virtue of their cute accent and frigid manners. It is, indeed, a constant source of gratification to the Englishman in America, no doubt abroad because society at home was intolerable, to be gratuitously endowed with these semimythical qualities propagated by Lord Byron and the wild-oat sowers. It is pleasant to be considered romantic on the strength of racial impassivity, cultivated on the strength of a dialect, and classy on the strength of an unknown background. The English have to be grateful for their semimythical compatriots, who thus dazzled or fooled the world into thinking them not only unhuman but uncommon. All that those who came after have to do to perpetuate the legend is to brush their hair flat, keep their faces rigid, and say "Quite!" with the air of finality usually expected only of the last trump.

III

The Real Thing. Genuine English Types

THE Gentleman. There is no denying the existence of a distinct English type known throughout the world under the term "gentleman." Most languages have neither the word nor the person. Even in America, where many English words and some English grammar are used, the expression "gentleman" is something of an importation, which has never become completely acclimatized. It is usually coupled with some more positive classification, such as "a scholar and a gentleman" or "ladies and gentlemen," but it could not be accurately employed to designate a businessman or a politician. The obvious reason for this is the significance of the English classification gentleman, which till recently was as much a profession as a mode of behavior.

Women novelists of the late nineteenth century tended to break down the social requirements implicit in the traditional gentleman, emphasizing the purely romantic qualities. Miss Craig's novel, *John Halifax, Gentleman*, for instance, changed social history by endowing a tanner with those attributes of character, courtesy, grace, and the rest, usually reserved for men of means and leisure. Thus it is that second-rate fiction, like popular science and journalistic rhetoric, may determine human destiny more than the historians, artists, and philosophers in general would care to admit; and we may be governed more by our superficial emotions and judgments than by the scrupulous, objective evaluations worked out with great pains in lecture hall, study, and laboratory.

Thus did a novelist whose primary appeal was to sex-starved seamstresses bring about a change in the social structure. From the publication of *John Halifax, Gentleman*, any Englishman with a tendency to solemnity, delayed action, and pigskin gloves could be called a gentleman. It was even possible for him, in literature at least, neither to speak with a refined accent nor to turn out to be a nobleman's bastard, to achieve this commendable status, particularly if his responses to such primitive and impolite needs as those of self-preservation and self-defense were a bit sluggish. Lowly Englishmen who stood on burning decks for patriotic reasons or who jumped into millponds to save the miller's sixteenth child or who died, like Tennyson's six hundred, to vindicate somebody else's blunder, were each speeded on his way to heaven by a grateful nation's cry, "He was a gentleman." The possibility of sheer stupidity or foolhardiness or bewilderment is not given much, if any, consideration. The English laud eccentricity in their dead with as much fervor as they require conformity in the living.

The English gentleman, then, is no longer necessarily a person of private means, such as a parson without an incumbency, a writer without any source of publication, or a parliamentarian without a seat. Character and, to some extent, appearance are the things that count today. The chief quality of character is self-abnegation, a standard derived from the conduct of those not-successful parsons, writers, and politicians of former days. This self-abnegation is manifested in the amazing and unpardonable politeness which both maddens and terrifies continental—and even American—observers. The gentleman in order to play his part must have no ideas, no opinions, and no criticisms. He must acquiesce, if not in words, then with a gracious smile, which acquiescence he can reverse in his own good time. For the gentleman must not tell a lie, unless it is to sacrifice his reputation for somebody else. This sacrificial zeal is tantamount, since the gentleman is the outcome of a bourgeois interpretation of Puritanism.

For practical purposes, the English gentleman is to be distinguished and recognized by his polish. On the whole, life offers few opportunities to march out of a tent at the South Pole, saying "Good night, gentlemen" or to dive off the Tower Bridge or to get one's reputation ruined for the gratification of a beautiful woman with the morality of a hungry jaguar; on the whole, we spend most of our time at office desks, trying to get rid of the representatives of philanthropic organizations, or at meal tables, assuring our wives that we don't mind hearing that story about the colored girl again. But these are the very occasions when the gentleman is seen in his true colors or, rather, when his polish is most brilliant and impressive. And these are the occasions whereon the English gentleman excels, whereon the type is unmistakable.

Those foreigners in England, who, after sitting in an outer room for three quarters of an hour, are finally ushered into the third secretary's office at a government department, know the quintessence of the English gentleman. Everything that one has to say is listened to with such exquisite attention that the lies or excuses one had prepared stick out like howitzers from a church window; and, as one continues, even the truth seems mean and trivial. The English gentleman is so immaculately dressed that the visitor is in agony because he shaved last night instead of this morning, and because black shoes do look pretty shoddy with a brown suit. The English gentleman is inviolate with his smooth, straw-colored hair, his pale eyes, his long face, his small moustache, and something which looks like a very distinguished old school tie. His accent is so cultivated, his grammar so impeccable, that the visitor stumbles blindly about in an agony of "between him and I," "more than us," collective nouns, singular verbs, adverbs with or without -ly, and the rest of it. Meanwhile, the Englishman, if he is a gentleman, will not bat an eyelid, but will be so sympathetically smiling that the visitor will positively know himself to be a country bumpkin. Then, feeling resentful, he may try another tack, making his address aggressive or jocular. Almost imperceptibly, the English gentleman freezes up, his smile grows fainter, and a quizzical line plays round the corner of his lips. In the presence of so much polish politeness, and savoir-faire, the visitor will break his ship on the rocks of his own submerged emotions, while the Englishman will sail lightly away unscathed.

33

For those who have not attempted to board the gentleman under these circumstances, but who wish to recognize him in order to avoid such temerity on their part, the type may be singled out on the London streets by a neat appearance, a clean, angular face, an upright carriage, an expression of polite indifference, and a neatly rolled umbrella. This latter is hooked over the arm when sauntering. A handkerchief is carried in the cuff. And—unmistakable evidence of a gentleman— you will feel vulgar and uncouth the moment you speak to him.

The Gentleman Boor or "Gent." The foreigner should attempt to distinguish, as the Englishman can distinguish, between the Polished Gentleman and the Gentleman Boor or, as the humble Englishman would call him, the Gent. The historically-minded will see in the gent the descendant of the squire, the nobleman in homespuns who, in his turn, bore definite resemblances to his even more ferocious Norse ancestors.

The English gent, in contrast to the polished gentleman, is not distinguished for any such qualities as grace, tact, and knowledge of the correct way to fold an umbrella. He would scorn with much more impatience than an American coal heaver the stuffing of a handkerchief under his cuff. For the gent is a conservative of the true-blue school. He has no time for fiddle-faddles, such as telephones, typewriters, and wrist watches. In military matters, in which he specializes with all the ferocity of a club-chair soldier, he still thinks airplanes are noisy toys and believes that an army, to be effective, should be slow and heavy, like a battleship.

The observer should have no difficulty at all in recognizing English gents. If he is unfortunate enough to sit opposite one in a railway carriage, he must expect to be fastened by a ferocious glare, intensified betimes by a single eyeglass. The inspection finished, the gent will retire behind the *Times* or the *Morning Post* with a half-suppressed snort. The paper is bound to be one or the other of these ponderous journals; for when the foreigner has the courage to return his gaze in the direction of the gent, he will notice how well the latter is screened off from the world by his large, staid sheet. He is, indeed, shut completely off, because the *Times* and the *Morning Post* are careful to avoid all suggestion of anything new happening in the world by devoting the front page to advertisements—not to any crude, clamorous announcements of a cure for halitosis or an incentive to foolhardiness through inhalation of a particular brand of cigarettes, but small, discrete, personal statements, such as "Si pacem vis, bellum para.— Patriae Amator"; or "Lord, we beseech thee, grant thy people grace to withstand the temptations of the world, the flesh, and the devil"; or, "Can B. J. remember the promise? I am waiting. Patience." Besides these strong expressions of British emotion, our eminent organs of respectability make certain concessions to trade of the more sober variety. "Beach Hotel," they announce, "Moderate rates. Five minutes from the sea. Quiet company. Discreet service. Excellent cuisine."

Behind this front, which effectively sobers all vulgar curiosity, the gent reads his own deep-seated convictions couched in the language he considers literary. There is

no nonsense about this kind of journalism. Americanisms, if used, are put in quotation marks, generally with
an air of indignation which elicits a snort from the right
side of the paper, but sometimes with a very sly dig.
" . . . or, as our American friends would say, 'we
don't mean perhaps!'" The gent will likely consider
this a "good one," though he will have to puzzle over
it for some time, and, if a purist, he may be annoyed to
the extent of writing a "letter to the *Times*."

Sir, In these times of compulsory and largely useless
elementary education, when our children leave school with
just enough reading ability to devour film journals, is it
prudent for your paper, long a stronghold of correct English,
to pander to vulgar taste in the direction of cheap
Americanisms?

I am, etc.,
Pro Lingua Pura.

Let the foreign critic in his observations upon and
analysis of the English gent, carefully note the "letters
to the *Times*," for hundreds of middle-aged Englishmen
of this class spend their lives writing to the *Times*. The
first thrush near London is noted regularly every year.
Gents in clubs watch the calendar eagerly for the
seasonal arrival of all the national flora and fauna. They
pounce upon every variance in traditional procedure.
No detail, from the derivation of a word to the omission
of their names from the telephone book, is overlooked
as the excuse for a "letter to the *Times*." Occasionally
the whole English gentry are hurling terrific recriminations at opponents over Chaucer's usage of an adjec-
tive, some pouncing with fiendish delight on an omission

in the *New English Dictionary*, others raising hypothetical eyebrows in huge arcs of suggested scorn at the error of *Lexicographer* or *Palaeologos* in last Tuesday's issue. Such controversy and polemics will not cease until news of a robin seen in Trafalgar Square or of a new theory for avoiding colds by massaging one's ears is used by a discreet editor to change a month-old topic.

Gents, then, don't have polish so much as bluster, snorts, and peeves. Their dress is not so irreproachable nor their grammar so impeccable as the gentleman's. However, they have an air. To the English workingman, for instance, there is no mistaking a gent, nob, swell, or toff, as he indiscriminately calls them. The foreigner will quickly learn to recognize them in their own country. They don't get abroad much, because in their opinion all foreigners are dirty, lecherous, or presumptuous. They don't like the Americans for the latter reason, except the American girls, who will find themselves extremely popular, possibly a little too popular for their own peace of mind. It should be remembered that a gent, having no conception whatever of an American, is quite sure that all American girls mate as freely as the birds.

Gents can be seen best in clubs and first-class railway carriages. Where else they go has not yet been discovered, unless they are ultimately lost forever in the pages of *Punch*, where the historian can find them glaring out from every second page, sharing the honors, indeed, with the homely housemaid and the oldest inhabitant of the village.

The Clerk. The English clerk stands secure on a basis of a secondary-school education and a refined accent. He is no shopkeeper, since that squeamishness which periodically affects the American language, transforming a bull into a "gentleman cow" and a shop assistant into a "clerk," has not erased the social distinctions between commerce and trade in England. A clerk is a clerk. He works in an office from nine till six, and his tool is a pen, not a sugar shovel.

Sometimes one feels in England the gloomy conviction that the nation has become a race of clerks. The world is completely theirs from eight till ten in the morning and from five till seven at night. The smooth electric trains which shoot into London, bring them in thousands from their boxlike homes—"Mon Repos," "Hillside," "Sunset View"—in the suburbs. And every clerk is the same in appearance, the same in manner, and the same in thought as every other.

The average foreigner will never have seen a clerk. Clerks do not go abroad, and the foreigner will not be up and about when they are migrating in seasonal swarms toward or away from London. They by no means resemble American businessmen or continental petty officials. They are neither so pudgy as the former nor yet so seedy as the latter. All traces of clerking have been meticulously removed from their appearance. There is neither ink on their fingers nor pouches under their eyes, so the observer might take an isolated specimen as an example of a gentleman, for they are more like gentlemen than like gents. Their dress, their air, their speech have similar characteristics. But if one makes a more careful examination, variant traits will be apparent. Look first, for instance, at the turn-ups of their striped trousers. Definitely a little frayed. Look next at the point where the shirt disappears into the waistcoat. A little grubby and darned. Glance, when opportunity allows, at the coat elbows and the trouser seat. Both shine. Drop the eye swiftly to the boots. Under their blacking they are cracked.

This ruthless prying may sound snobbish or cruel, but one need have no compunction over hurting the feelings of clerks on these scores. Clerks can erect barriers of their own snobbishness and mental indifference which make them impregnable to criticism, for the object of this unhuman and frigid appearance of theirs is simply to assert their superiority not only to all other clerks, but to the rest of the world as well. The evidence, then, of certain human qualities, such as shiny seats and grammatical mistakes, may actually endear them a little more to people who are human to the extent of buying new clothes, even if they can't afford them, and to people who don't mind wearing old ones. It is well, that is, to have a peep behind the clerical mask— well for one's peace of mind. Otherwise, the observer must conclude that England is populated by twenty million automata, apparently brought to London every morning from cells somewhere in the country.

The clerk, however, has a domestic life. First of all, and above all, he has a home: a new home with six rooms, a bath, a garage, a garden sixty feet long—two hundred pounds down and thirty shillings a week for ten years. In this home lives a person referred to by *Punch* as "the little woman." The little woman, it is noticeable, generally overtops her husband by a couple of inches and upholds the general conception of the Englishwoman as tall, angular, and flatfooted. *Real* little women are also found in clerks' homes, most of them with thin noses and rimless spectacles. The green grocer is in great awe of these.

The ambition of every clerk is to have a car. Any visitor who has walked along those desolate new roads lined with hideous £800 houses will have seen little square cars standing outside of the front gates. These cars could not have meant much to him, unless he was aware of their clerical significance. He would suppose, no doubt, that they are for riding about in—going down to the grocer's, calling on the Joneses—although the American would suspect them of being pretty uncomfortable for any distance. But these vehicles are not, as a matter of fact, so much for riding in as for looking at. They represent a $1,250 investment, which is partially the explanation of the frayed cuffs, shiny seats, and skimpy lunches characteristic of clerks.

Cars in England are not so much to be used as polished. Everyone in the family polishes the car, and as one walks down Sunray Avenue on a Sunday morning, one can see the male members of the families polishing their machine in the garage. About 11:30 A.M., the car is taken out of the garage and stood outside the front-room window. Passers-by, as well as the neighbors, can thus appreciate it. Sometimes, after lunch, it is taken for a "run around." The clerk drives with many signals and lofty comments on pedestrians. Dogs are slowed down for, and a beam of loving-kindness overspreads everybody's face as they are allowed to trot, at their own leisure, across the road. The clerk's wife occasionally lets out a cry of alarm as a corner is taken at twenty-five miles an hour and another car approaches at thirty. The children say in their prim secondary-school accents, "Don't go on like that, mother."

The car is a symbol of security and respectability. These two states are the end of clerks in this world, with modest but unquestioned expectations that they will be continued in the next.

The Worker. Foreign visitors have usually found the English worker a peculiarly depraved or brutalized individual. Most of them, such as Emerson, Marx, and Taine, pitied the state of the working classes, and supposed that it could be improved. Marx's harrowing evidence concerning working-class conditions, it will be recollected, gave body and weight to *Das Kapital* and a crusading spirit to all communists. Taine, the French literary critic, was equally affected in his way by the conditions he saw in the slums of London. He would have seen worse, had he gone to the Midlands. To this day foreign observers can see in England millions of people living in surroundings so poverty-stricken and dismal that one questions the economic soundness and the social morality that permit such a state of affairs. Most of these millions constitute the workers, a type as far removed from the English gentleman, who apparently typifies the Englishman abroad, as a Japanese coolie is from a lieutenant in the German Navy.

The English worker, in common with his continental brothers, does not dissemble his appearance, as the clerk dissembles his. Moreover, unlike his American counterpart, he permanently and continuously evinces his social status. He cannot, that is, be a workman from eight till six, and an ordinary, well-dressed, socially acceptable citizen after hours. He changes his clothes only on Sundays and Bank Holidays, and even then in a single glance he can be recognized for what he is. His first word will confirm the impression, moreover, for he can never escape the evidence of either his labor or his accent. The former is written in his creased face and coarsened hands; the latter is heard in every vowel he uses; so that, if the foreigner sees on Sunday an individual with a cap worn flat toward the front of the head, a choker instead of a collar and tie around his neck, and a pair of boots down at the heel, he will know immediately that it is a workingman, somewhat uncomfortable in his Sunday clothes. And if the individual is heard to say, "Well, mayte, wot abaht a quick one dahn at Ted's?" the listener can conclude that he has heard a phrase of genuine Cockney.

The English middle class have long considered the working classes low, depraved, and undernourished by nature and by preference. Toward the end of the nineteenth century, when the country was incredibly affluent, the condition of this "very numerous and interesting portion of the population," as they were referred to in Parliament, became something of a sore to the eyes of those upright citizens who were robbed on their way to church or knocked down in attempting to collect the rents on their slum properties. Hence, various reforms in the nature of patches to cover these social sores were proposed and passed by a beneficent government. In 1850 public libraries were built as rivals to the public houses, although unfortunately the local authorities were not permitted to spend anything on books. These were donated by wealthy citizens during the annual clearance of attics and cellars. Crumbling hymnbooks and volumes of sermons poured into the public libraries, and these, together with the auto-biographies of the more successful tradesmen, were supposed to act as a counterattraction to the particularly potent brew of the period. Moreover, the working classes of the England of 1850 could not read, and in any case they had no time for reading, as they worked fourteen hours a day and had to take turns in the common beds, as they had a chance.

In looking at the English workingman, the foreign observer should remember that the knobby and some-what malformed artisan has materially pulled himself up by his own bootstraps. His forefathers began to get a bit of education about 1880; and he himself left school at the age of fourteen, never to receive any formal instruction or refinement afterwards. Hence, he is to some extent brutalized. His appearance in choker and cap, the manner in which his lower lip hangs low, and the formidable language which rasps from his mouth as he falls back on the sexual and excrementory functions to emphasize his opinion, all make him not only "curious and interesting," but sometimes positively un-pleasant. On the other hand, the very absence of those satisfying conditions which sustain the clerk and the gentleman—respectability and security—gives to the workingman some of the casual humor we find in other unprovided and improvident groups.

The English workingman is both casual and good-humored. With all the time in the world, he never keeps an appointment. If invited out as a special treat by some nob, swell, or toff, he will arrive three-quarters of an hour late for dinner, not out of fashionableness, but from a complete unawareness of the tyranny of time. His own meals come irregularly, and it doesn't worry him overmuch when they come, as long as there is finally a suet pudding, gray and doughy, plumped on the table. The workingman's idea of luxury is a salacious newspaper in bed on Sunday morning, a trip down to the pub before dinner, a mutton chop at three o'clock or thereabouts, a snooze after the meal, a big tea at five o'clock, and a visit to the pictures with "the old woman" at night.

If the foreigner wishes to see the real workingman, let him examine the bus drivers, the railway porters, and the perpendicular drinkers in London's waterside pubs. He might remember, too, that the dignified London copper is a workingman in a uniform, and that in the next war most of the Tommies will be the workers too.

The Student. It is often easy to tell what people are by the way they walk or stand or sit. The English student indicates his pursuits by the way he sits, marked preference being shown for a semirecumbent position, with the weight evenly distributed along the spine and coming to rest somewhere near the nape of the neck. The legs project far into the room or the public conveyance, and are enveloped in baggy, uncreased, gray trousers. Above the trousers is a sports coat—a brown tweed coat, which is never changed, never cleaned, and never pressed. The face of the English student is lean and often bespectacled. The detective of types should look for the characteristic university extension nobs on the forehead. No hat is worn unless it has been duly battered beyond resemblance to any headgear worn by men not engaged in the pursuit of knowledge.

All English students—and it should be pointed out here that in England the term applies only to men attending a university; the others are schoolboys—all English students are, in the large terminology of American newspapers, "reds." The more studious and brilliant they are, the redder they may be expected to be. Thus it is that, in selecting the cream of them to study abroad, the American philanthropic foundations are yearly bringing to these shores a group of ardent young communists, armed with the force of dialectics and the grace of well-cultivated personalities. William Randolph Hearst in attacking the Foundations as un-American, is evincing, therefore, the remarkable perspicacity which has helped him to mold the American destiny. His logic in condemning the pursuit of truth as subversive is infallible, and by the same token he is justified in anathematizing it to the utmost of his ability.

To those who, like bulls, find red a disturbing color, there is comfort in the knowledge that British paternalism is in no way perturbed by student oaths or activities. To the contrary, the future rulers and administrators of the Empire choose their successors from the reddest of the reds on the simple assumption that they are, ipso facto, the best minds available among the younger generation. All the scolding that needs be done is undertaken by the gents referred to above. The gents will write letters to the *Times*, menace the students from club chairs, threaten to cut off allowances, clamor for reprisals against Russia, and grow the color they abhor over their port wine and cigars.

In the meantime, the gentlemen in the government watch with amused unconcern the antics of the October

Club and the student paraders. No doubt they themselves, once upon a time, carried banners in a procession, attempted to teach workingmen how to play "rugger," and wrote articles for magazines mimeographed in their own homes. They realize with an inner conviction that the squat, powerful pillar of English society cannot be overthrown by the mental pyrotechnics of a group of young men, any more than the police system is endangered by periodical student "rags," when the total damage will amount to not more than £20 in broken glass and a few sore heads next morning.

The English student is a type who is fairly real and human even to the foreigner. He drifts about America in fairly large numbers, bewildering the inhabitants of small towns with his varicolored costume and incomprehensible accent. This latter, it should be observed, is as much a handicap to the speaker as to the listener; hence the slight stutter which often characterizes the best English English. The English student, in spite of the incipient frigidity which will enfold him in later life, metamorphosing him into an English gentleman, is eager to be human and likable. He is a bit shy, however, and has to struggle against the unhuman attributes with which he is inculcated at home. Because of this, he is carried completely off his feet when treated as a human being, and, while feeling as though he would like to break down and cry, usually marries, instead, the first American girl who asks him.

The Adventurer. On transatlantic liners one will generally find an English adventurer, usually traveling third class. Such an individual will not *always* be the kind to touch you for a "fivah," until he can cash a check. Even if he does this, he should be humored into free drinks and cigarettes for the yarns he can spin during the dog watch. For there is a type of Englishman, a variety of adventurer who decorates the beaches of subtropical islands between occasional spells of wandering all over this still-undiscovered earth, whose stories, being as skillful as his begging, should be encouraged; for the listener will see in such an individual the Englishman who has made an empire possible. Not an empire of Manchester cotton goods, Sheffield cutlery, and Pasternoster Row Bibles; but an empire of exploration, of hard conquest under an equatorial sun, and of small administrative posts in Gambia. Sometimes the foreigner will have the good fortune to meet a British colonial civil servant, or a wandering journalist, or an insatiable explorer. From such men the major English traits of respectability and security and smugness have been stripped away, and the bleak, sterling characteristics remain, as the fine bone structure of the face remains after the fatty deposits of comfort and luxury have been burned away by whisky and an African sun.

Here is one on the *Berengaria*, a third-class passenger from Southampton to New York. He comes down to breakfast on the first morning with an awful hangover from the night before. He speaks to no one save the little Jewish doctor who is returning from a year in Budapest. He is no snob, then; on the contrary, he seeks out all those third-class passengers whom the more respectable of the travelers, in their attempt to salvage their bourgeois dignity, have decided to avoid.

The adventurer is six feet something in his socks. He stoops a little from constant efforts to bring himself down to lesser heights. He is short-sighted, having read

much by candlelight—particularly the Greek drama-
tists. Besides, his glasses are a social asset, he observes.
They hide his eyes and real feelings from other people.
He intimates that he holds an administrative post on
the Gold Coast—lives in the interior, the only white
man for miles. He awoke one morning to remember he
had promised an American girl he would marry her and
has traveled six thousand miles to do so, though he's
damned if he knows why. He is a person of keen wit and
long silences. He, too, is unhuman in his way, but in
such a way that all those who come into contact with
him wish they could be unhuman too. One will never
see him again, except in the mind's eye before dropping
off to sleep, when he will be reading Aeschylus somewhere by the banks of a river in Africa.

The Exile.   The exile might be described as the adventurer gone to seed; he has the desire but not the will
to adventure. He dislikes and avoids his countrymen as
individuals, but endorses the British Empire most
heartily when they are not around. He retains the most
English characteristics: the voice, the clothes, and the
traditions. For some psychological reason he even
retains his British citizenship, although he never expects to return to his native shores. Why he left England and does not return, nobody knows, but one
envisions a wife and three children somewhere in the
suburbs of London. Hotel maids suspect him of being a
spy, and this is possible, but unlikely; for he never goes
anywhere nor does anything, except to play tennis and
chess.

Americans never regard him as English, except to
note his unfortunate accent. Passing Englishmen can

tell a lot from this, for it is usually of a synthetic variety, with a pseudo-Oxonian speech grafted onto a strong Cockney stock. Obviously the exile never got further than an elementary school nor rose higher in the ranks than a military batman. To the American the exile has a fair degree of success and status. To the English visitor he is a pitiful failure. Each of them knows that the other knows this. So the exile retires into himself until such time as the stranger has gone away, when he emerges with an accent more strongly Oxonian and a patriotism even more fervent. He can be recognized by these two traits, since the genuine Englishman abroad is modest with regard to his accent and imperialism, recognizing both as encumbrances.

IV

Specimens Continued. Females

IT APPEARS to be true that the women of any society fall into broader and more general groups than the men. Their nature, conduct, objectives, and professions are largely common to the whole sex. It is scarcely necessary to point in evidence of this fact to the recency of their so-called emancipation, which gave them a voice in government, a share in education, and the opportunity to follow some profession other than maternity. In spite of these concessions, the age-old forces and influences which determined women's status and very lives are still quietly effective today. Their own psychology has not kept pace with their liberty, and they have, and can have, no emancipation until they free themselves of their own mental and emotional limitations.

All very smug, of course; all old potatoes to intelligent women. Those of them who have had the determination to deny the bondage of sex with as inflexible (albeit a quieter) insistence as that with which their mothers repudiated the economic peonage, will say with pardonable bitterness that they have proved their independence of the self-appointed lords of creation; but all the time, as much today as a thousand years ago, this feverish business of getting themselves pursued and irrefutably captured occupies the attention of women in general. It disintegrates their education, spoiling the fun of wooing knowledge in an old coat by a midnight lamp; it gnaws at their professional efficiency, limiting them to manual jobs like typing, in order that their minds may be left free to concentrate on their appearance; and it enslaves their whole social existence to the inexorable necessity of looking their best. The powder puff still dominates a woman's life. A female with an uncomely face may escape—unless she has a good figure. Only the old and friendless can really enjoy living for living's sake, and then only after they have broken the habit of a half century's titivation.

All these things hold true of English as of American or any other women, except that between the English and the American there is a difference in emphasis. American women have lightened their task by making the means an end. A pretty appearance, in England a means, is in America an end in itself. In other words, American women, while spending more time on their appearance than any other women in the world (with the possible exception of the women in Mohammedan seraglios), achieve a result which justifies the pains as another consummation devoutly to be wished and as an end sufficient in itself. The result of this bold exploitation of limitations on the part of American women has been to oblige the men to modify their behavior accordingly.

American women take their triumph and tribute in the form of male attention. The male is demoted from a cavalier to an attendant, from a lover to a customer, from a husband to a factor. Thus, in spite of the manifestly unfair odds, the lighter, fleeter regiments of American women have by their cunning strategy trapped the whole masculine forces. It might be observed, however, that they have achieved this remarkable victory only by strict regimentation and implicit obedience according to the dictates of sex. They have escaped the domination of men only to fall into the clutches of their own inferior natures. They have given up guerilla warfare for feminine dictatorship; and, as we are led to expect of dictatorship, we find a fairly uniform type with a high standard of physical attractiveness but a low standard of mental vigor. There are among American women only a few rebels who dwell apart in the fastnesses of their own personalities and carry on the war for feminine freedom.

English women, on the whole, have not developed so good an organization and such effective strategy. They are much too conservative to realize the advantage of a united front. For one thing their enemy, while smaller in numbers, is correspondingly elusive; and for another, the prizes of conquest are neither so numerous nor so desirable. Women outnumber men in England, which is an initial psychological disadvantage. In some places there are as many as ten females to one male—a condition which fosters a defeatist frame of mind to the extent of almost condoning concubinage.

Then, there is a whole generation of English women who have been deprived of even the satisfaction of battle: the war took the energies, the bitter-sweet hostility, and the lives of the men they might have carried off as their conquering captives. This generation of middle-aging women, thousands of them, stands as an awful warning to the rest. The old ones suddenly realize the values of security, respectability, and the status that matrimony implies, and throw their weight behind the conservative bloc. Marriage and the subordination of women, they declare, must continue. Women are inferior, the "weaker vessels," fashioned only for the comfort and solace of man. The younger women modify the rebellion and expectation of youth, and desert surreptitiously to the ranks of the enemy. And so, while women in England have the dubious satisfaction of partial emancipation, they have been psychologically and spiritually driven back to their old positions of earlier centuries.

In view of their common cause and common disasters, it will be seen now that women can be spoken of in more generalized terms than men. Similarly, they can be classified into larger and more comprehensive groups, since the emotional characteristic far transcends the economic and professional, used to describe the Englishmen.

Englishwomen fall into three classes: married women, spinsters, and girls; and types will be analyzed in this account accordingly.

Married Women. There is no mistaking the English married woman, the mother in particular, as far as her appearance is concerned; for the English mother is still very much the housewife—a cook, a seamstress, a maker of beds, a scrubber of floors, and a washerwoman.

These duties leave their imprint on her face and hands. Not that she is necessarily bent and worn in appearance; that will depend on her constitution. But there will be something in her manner and appearance to manifest the years of loving drudgery within the confines of a house. Her position is, after all, that of a servant.

If the household is an affectionate one, her bondage is transmuted into a willing service; and it has its compensations, which increase with the years, so that motherhood in this domestic sense is one of the ultimate and unchanging human values. "Mother!" shout father and son, "where are my clean shirts?" Nobody else, neither wife nor servant nor laundryman, can be shouted at like this; the English mother is used to it, and is not aggrieved. It is a strange business—a business which those women who revolt against the bondage forced upon their sex in the name of affection will deplore. The English mother, however, would be the last one either to deplore or to change it. Having been shouted at, having run for the shirt and ironed the collar, having hung the garment in front of the fire to warm, having threaded the cuff links to prevent the oaths from becoming too strong and too loud, the mother admires the fully dressed man, is pleased that he is going out, and settles down to finish the pile of undarned socks.

In the more rosy literature and films the mother receives ample reward for her sacrifice. Husbands bring flowers, children many a little surprise. Lips and hands are extended in touches of appreciation. Better still, the mother accompanies the handsome son to the important social function, and he sticks to her among a whole roomful of comely young women. In real life, the average English mother with three or more children receives few compensations for her surrender. The sons from whom she could naturally get the most satisfying return are as naturally fretful of yielding it. To them "mum" is, in retrospect, a dear. They would defend her, support her, and so forth. But they go away when they want to, to get a better job, to marry, to travel. There is little return from them. English daughters are more dutiful and more affectionate. They stay at home more, help their mothers, and manifest numerous little tokens of affection which the menfolk are constantly overlooking. But one woman can seldom satisfy the emotional needs of another. No mother would consider in her heart a daughter's affection sufficient to recompense for the pangs of childbirth and the years of bondage her position has entailed. It is a man's admiration she wants; first a husband's, then a son's.

The English married woman's happiness will be in proportion to the satisfaction of this need; and her appearance, in its turn, will depend on her happiness. These conditions no doubt hold true for women in general, except to the extent that women have independent sources of gratification. American women have numerous sources of this kind: professional ambition, personal appearance, and club activities among them. The last two, which are the most significant in American life, are those most often lacking in the case of the English. The English married woman, in contrast to her American counterpart, pays very little attention to her appearance. Probably not one of a thousand middle-class English married women ever visits a beauty specialist. It is quite a breath-taking adventure to have their hair cut short, and they undergo the most severe moral qualms in getting it washed or waved by somebody else. Only the very rich and volatile have their nails manicured by a professional. If their eyebrows are plucked, this is done in the privacy of their own rooms, when there is no question that everyone else is out for the afternoon. Then with secret elation and delicious pain the adventurer removes the most obtrusive hairs, hoping that everyone will notice the general improvement and no one the particular cause.

It is natural that middle-aged Englishwomen should compensate in some way for the absence of aids to beauty, such as cosmetics. They are permitted a little powder, but lip rouge is taboo. Not being allowed to run to marcel waves, eyebrow plucking, face lifting, nail enameling, and like methods of titivation frowned upon by Presbyterianism, the English married woman shows a marked predilection for such adornment as is permitted, notably necklaces, bracelets, earrings, and broaches. Many an English mother compensates for her deprivations by frequent visits to Woolworth's; and a drawer full of knickknacks, which prim daughters have constantly to restrain their mothers from using, testifies to this secret vice.

English middle-aged women, whether married or not, are by no means smart in appearance. The odds are too heavy against them, for in addition to the displeasure of a conservative society, they have to contend with a disagreeable climate and unimaginative tailors in their efforts to look attractive. A conservative society forbids them to introduce too radical aids toward improving their faces; a disagreeable climate necessitates warm and voluminous clothing; and unimaginative tailors put all the value into the cloth and none into the cut. Thus it is that we have a type of middle-aged Englishwoman without make-up, dressed in unprovocative tweeds, and shod as though with the express purpose of making her feet look as large as possible. All Englishwomen give up the struggle from the knees downward. With inferior and expensive brands of artificial silk stockings, with low-heeled brogue shoes, their calves bulge and shine unduly, and their feet have a dull, tired appearance. It was long thought in Europe that Englishmen could not be knocked down because, like toy Humpty-Dumpties, they were weighted at the bottom. It is still considered impossible to carry an Englishwoman off her feet.

It might be concluded from these statements that married Englishwomen have a very thin time compared to their American sisters. That will depend on one's values. It is possible to be just as happy making a suet pudding as listening to a talk on Japanese flower gardens. Let us say, it is possible to be as satisfied with a lot to do as with nothing much to do, which might in general be stated to be the principal difference between the average English and American middle-class housewife.

As far as expression (in contrast to grooming) is concerned, the Englishwoman seems to come off better. Her appearance, in proportion as it is less metallic, is likewise less forbidding. The constant labor of love which absorbs her life throws over her face a veil of kindliness and repose, which compensates, in a way, for the ebbing

57

of beauty. Her gray hairs inspire affection as well as respect. If she possesses a generous bosom, this gives an impression of comfort rather than serving as an indication of club presidentship. Old age in England, therefore, has its compensations, whereas in America it is liable to have only regrets.

The Spinsters. Human society likes to have certain groups or professions as whipping horses for its discontent with its own mediocrity. In America schoolteaching is one of the despised professions; in England, librarianship. The spinsters form an uncommended group in both countries. In America a spinster is really a rather extraordinary person, either by not wanting or not being able to marry. It is quite understandable in these cases that a person who does not or cannot comply with the requirements of the herd is an object of social suspicion. People more innocuous than spinsters, whether American or English, are hard to be found; but these large stipulations laid down by the race take little cognizance of individual tastes where a common good is envisaged, the common good, in this case, being the stabilization of society through the home and the propagation of the species by marriage.

The English spinster is not to blame for her isolation and loneliness. The war took some husbands, the depression others. Anyone who compares the marrying age of the Americans and the English may notice with what gusto and improvidence the former rush into it, how sober and cautious are the latter. Several fairly obvious factors explain this discrepancy. The American woman's superior sex technique, resulting from her concern with her appearance, is one. On the other side, while the young Englishman earns far less than an American of comparable age and qualifications, marriage entails a far greater economic responsibility. It entails "setting up home"—buying a house, if possible, furnishing it, and giving the appearance, at least, of security and respectability. Because of these last requirements, the wife must not work (in many cases the regulations will not permit her to). The man must earn enough for two. Again, as a married couple, the English pair, although still young, cannot live the mobile, irresponsible existence of their youth. For this reason, English students seldom marry till their studies are finished. They are finished at about twenty-five years of age, when the graduate emerges into the world without any assets but his diploma. He can reckon on another five years before he can support a wife. He marries, then, at about thirty.

What happens to the English girl in the meantime? She waits. And since the English prematrimonial period is strictly monogamous, she is limited to a single chance. A certain staleness and inevitability creep into the man-and-girl relationship, which irks the man and depresses the girl. The girl grows older, losing her freshness of face as well as of personality with the passage of the years. At the threshold of middle age, she may suddenly find herself confronted with spinsterhood. That not more English girls are so left is due more to most men's rather surly sense of honor (and fear of a breach of promise) than to their alacrity to get married. The English marriage of this delayed variety is neither a marriage of romance nor one of convenience. It is a marriage of habitude.

The body of English spinsters to be accounted for by reason of war, depression, and delay is quite large. The observer who accepts the popular belief that a spinster is the modern counterpart of a fourteenth-century witch will be surprised at the looks, charm, and intelligence of many of the English "old maids." If they come through their ordeal of frustration and censure unbroken, it may be assumed that they have considerable moral stamina, to say the least. They turn their energies into other channels. They are great readers and writers and include in their ranks some of the outstanding English novelists of today. Some join a cause. At the meetings of Sir Oswald Moseley's fascists it is usually the spinsters who rise in protest and are rough-handled for their pains. During the summer vacations they will be seen striding in pairs through the Black Forest or in the Austrian Tyrol. Foreigners laugh at their rough tweeds, their projecting teeth, their un-waved hair, and their flat-heeled shoes. But these women are used to being the subject of laughter. There is always another village tomorrow.

The need for some richer fulfillment than a job, a circle of friends, and the pleasures of the intellect does not die in them because of their sexual loneliness. From time to time it seems to them as though a dream is going to come true. A middle-aged widower is attentive throughout a sea trip and continues his attentions for a time by letter. Comes an invitation to meet him in some small seaside town. Clothes are bought, preparations made. A friend suggests that there might be something suspicious about the widower's offer. Inquiries are made. Yes, it was to be a hotel, a room with twin beds.

The mother on hearing of it, weeps copiously. It will ruin *her* life as well. The spinster, being not so much in love as in need, undergoes a short period of revolt. Why shouldn't she? What has she to lose? Then, sick of the whole thing, well aware of the shoddiness of the situation, she cancels the arrangement and hears no more from her "lover."

Those things should be remembered when observing and analyzing the English spinster. Such a woman is not a witch nor a monstrosity. She calls for no cheap jibes, and there is in the eagerness of her face and the cut of her sensible clothes more courage than can customarily be expected of the human race.

The Girls.   They are all supposed to have such lovely complexions, the English girls. The generalization seems only moderately accurate, which is no doubt all that can be expected. Actually, they have no great pretensions to good looks. Many of them are too gawky, and the passion for games overdevelops their calves and sense of sportsmanship. Nobody likes a sportsman-like girl; nor is there any point in her playing games so very efficiently. It is even more pointless than it would be in a man.

The best way for a foreigner to see English girls is not on advertisements for Palmolive soap, but at a girls' secondary school. In summer he will see them walking along demurely under undulating white straw hats. In winter the hats change from white straw to blue felt, the dresses from muslin to serge.

The English girl is characterized by her extreme naïveté and innocence. In her general attitudes this is expressed in a protracted tomboyishness. On occasions such as when dancing, something flutters within her, and she is likely to cling to her partner with charming affection. She will, indeed, fall deeply in love with any man over the age of twenty-five and under fifty-five who has the discretion to treat her with studied respect. Any mention of mysteries she does not understand—society conspiring to keep her in ignorance of all that matters in life—or any of the heavy methods successful on ripe Latin women, will cause her to shy away with horror; but a friendly, easy attitude combined with hair graying at the man's temples is irresistible to the English girl.

She is intelligent—far more so than youths of her own age, whom she very justly despises—well-behaved, and stimulating, the best possible companion for a long country walk. She will not have reached the striding, vigorous stage of her elder sister. She loves best of all to tease. There is no one in the world like the English schoolgirl for teasing.

Book II

SOCIETY

V

Democracy

FROM one of those postprandial platitudes which eventually assume from repetition a certain cabalistic significance, we learn that a country's laws are of little importance compared to its songs. In other words, we can judge what a people are more by what they sing than by what they are permitted to do. The theory is a romantic rather than psychological explanation of national conduct. This is clearly apparent in the case of the Negroes. Negroes, like birds, are inveterate songsters. They break into the spiritual and sing in chorus about happy lands far, far, away at the slightest provocation. The romanticist would interpret their singing as an indication of an irrepressible *joie de vivre;* the psychologist prefers a theory of compensation: lively imagination in lieu of a barren life.

In the case of the English, when they roar out in their national choruses that Britons never, never, never will be slaves, this might be taken as evidence either of an inner confidence or of a desperate need for self-assurance; they might be either reiterating the certainty of their freedom or, inversely, merely regretting the absence of it. We can supply our own interpretations of this in-

65

teresting phenomenon or accept the evidence at its face value, assuming that if a nation periodically bellows that it never, never, never will be slaves, it means it never will be slaves.

There can be no doubt that the history of the British race illustrates the people's firm resolve to be free—free, however, according to a certain interpretation of the word, according to a democratic way of life.

Be that as it may, English society has long been quietly yet firmly democratic, in contrast to American society, which is neither quiet nor firm. Democracy in England had a good, sober, bourgeois start, whereas in America it was a pretty wild and revolutionary experiment. English democracy knew for centuries what it wanted. It did not want every man a king overnight, and it did not want any wobbly liberalistic ideas about equality. It wanted two very practical objectives: a strong government at home and a free market abroad. These two objectives are the alpha and omega of English democracy. Upon the degree of their attainment and retention depends the stability of the English system. Unlike the Americans, the English evaluate democracy in terms of material advantages. While Americans fought for a common ideal and then diffused their inexhaustible energy in attempting to establish an individualistic type of freedom, the English fought for bigger territories and wider markets, afterwards glorified for ethical reasons in the ideas of empire and democracy. English democracy, it should be remembered, is not a political ideal but an economic necessity. It is the tradesman's conception of the most profitable economic and social organization.

English history since the Middle Ages has been the history of this commercial ideal, an ideal which necessitated first the overthrow of feudalism and then the substitution of economic freedom.

Let it be recalled that high finance, as much as money lending, was denied to all but the Jews throughout the Middle Ages. There was no economic freedom for either merchant or tradesman. No armed forces protected the former's goods on the high seas or other trade routes. It was a soldier's function to fight for Christendom rather than for commerce, so the tradesman had little freedom to cheat his customers by the democratic practices of selling underweight or adulterating his wares. The baker, in his economic bondage, threw in an extra loaf to the dozen to make sure he was within the law; and the innkeeper, with the prospect of a hangman's noose ahead, was afraid to dilute his beer with so much as a drop of water. So there was no freedom, in the democratic sense, in the Middle Ages.

The Civil War in England saw the overthrow of this economic bondage. Some historians interpret the events of the time as a triumph for personal freedom as well; but as a matter of fact, large groups of society were actually being deprived of their liberty in the change-over. Kings were being deprived of theirs, aristocrats of theirs, the peasants of theirs, for kings lost their autocracy, lords their temporal power, peasants their public lands. Moreover, they lost them to a new and comparatively small class in the social structure, the middle or merchant class. These men certainly gained a large measure of liberty—liberty to ignore the king, liberty to dictate to the lords, and liberty to draft, to mulct the peasants. These men, then, changed the face, the system, and the destiny of England. They changed it physically by covering it with factories and large centers of population where before there had been cottages and villages; they changed it socially by breaking down the old absolute hierarchy and substituting a democracy; and they changed it economically by introducing production for profit where before there had been production for use.

Most of this change was of a constitutional or evolutionary nature, as compared to the violent overthrow of existing governments in other parts of the world. The English enemies of the status quo made slow advances, consolidating their positions as they went. There was no driving them back as the rebels in other states were driven back. Where they needed a concession, they took the precaution of making it legal through an act of parliament. The opposing forces, those of the autocratic Stuarts, for instance, made the mistake of ignoring this elementary strategic principle of legality. The Stuarts omitted to legislate and attempted to collect taxes without the customary pious references to God and country. That the English have no objection to being mulcted for ends they do not approve or are not aware of, is apparent in their present system, whereby the government can collect twelve shillings in every pound without any difficulty at all.

Indeed, unbelievable as it may seem, the English wait in lines to pay their income taxes whenever the government proclaims a national emergency, which it does every fiscal year. To the Americans who shout of regimentation every time any social legislation is proposed, this must appear an impressive, nay, an almost depressing phenomenon. The French, with their inveterate cynicism in matters of government and taxes alike, regard it as pure hypocrisy, in keeping with the characteristic sanctimoniousness of the English people. But try to collect from an Englishman without first repeating a platitude, and he will immediately fortify his house like a castle and defy the world. It might be said, in brief, that he pays his taxes, as Samuel Butler asserted he worshiped God—for spite.

English democracy, having been slowly and cautiously evolved, is probably the soundest in the world. It is not an experiment with an idea, as most other European democracies are—democracies which, as in the case of the postwar states, collapse at the forceful jostling of another idea—but the realization of a need. The need, as we have seen, was primarily an economic one: the need for a free and wider market. At the same time, not even English tradesmen live by selling bread alone; they like the more practical and discreet assets of culture as well. They like order, not only in society at large, but in their home in particular. They like stability in both their government and their furniture. They like well-stored minds, as well as well-stored granaries. They like respectability of appearance, as well as orderly conduct. So these corollaries of democracy have been included within the English system. The merchant builds himself a large house, collects a library, and dresses like a gentleman. He atones for the economic bondage he has imposed on society by countenancing every kind of intellectual freedom. In no other country have so many revolutionary schemes, be they political, economic, scientific, or literary, been disseminated and discussed and adopted by minorities. Even the most revolutionary idea in the history of the world, that of communism, was worked out in the British Museum. And this is the strength and the steadfastness of English democracy; freedom in everything except in the means of life. Around the squat pillar of English middle-class society every kind of vine and creeper grows and flourishes. Within the heart of the Empire, in every public place in London, revolutionary doctrines are propagated and proved.

Those foreign observers who really wish to discover and feel for themselves the latitude and elasticity of British democracy should spend their lunch hours on Tower Hill and their evenings at Hyde Park Corner. There is a lot of irony in the choice of these two historic spots for the propagation of doctrines ranging from fascism to communism, from the liberalism of Catholic priests to the absolutism of Salvation Army professional repenters. On the whole, Tower Hill may be said to specialize in the "fighting parson" type of oratory; Hyde Park Corner, in political minorities, nicely seasoned with a spicing of what the Hearst press so neatly terms "crackpots."

In the shadow of the Tower and in the presence of who knows what distinguished shades, clerks listen to exhortations to find God through socialism—or socialism through God—the while they are placidly munching on their beef sandwiches. At Hyde Park a motley crowd of Cockneys, bored with Sunday evening, and red-coated soldiers, declaring their amorous propensities with the display of strutting peacocks, listen with divided attention to the almost mythical Charlie who for nearly twenty years has been "burning the question papers" every Wednesday and Sunday evening; to the advocate of birth control and his perennial joke at the expense of Moses in the bulrushes; to the Indian nationalists who convert each other regularly every Saturday afternoon; to the whining Salvation Army convert; to the Catholic socialist and the Catholic fascist; to the Trade Union speaker or the exponent of a new system of shorthand; and to a dozen or so other orators whose fists rise and fall in the dusk under the trees. Subversive doctrines are expounded, accepted, cheered every Saturday night. Occasionally the communists chase the fascists across the open spaces of the Park; or sometimes the police chase the communists.

But next Sunday morning the aristocracy of birth and wealth, harangued at, condemned, and demolished the previous evening, ride forth into Rotten Row and comely nursemaids wheel babies along the intersecting paths. The British system and English democracy are unchanged. The pillar of society, the extent of the Empire, and the conformation of the city are unaffected. Stone, territory, and buildings cannot be overthrown by words. Only guns and gunpowder can displace them, and until these means of destruction are used, English democracy will no doubt continue to support one third of the world. So strong is the inner conviction underlying this democracy that the stately English bobby opposes its enemies with nothing more than a truncheon—and seldom uses even that, on the universally accepted assumption among his fifty million fellow countrymen that right is stronger than might.

VI

The Class System

TO UNDERSTAND properly the nature of class distinctions in England today, it is necessary to know something about the historical factors which determined them in the past. It is sufficient for our purposes, however, to recognize the appearance of class in its modern conformation after the disruption of the medieval hierarchy, remembering that this disruption was largely due to the rise of the new middle classes, for four centuries the revolutionary element in society, strange as that may sound in an age of more sudden and catastrophic revolutions. But, strange or not, we know that it was the merchant class which engineered and carried through the Civil War in England, and fought the established social order on numerous other occasions. As individualists and liberals, these dissenters, both religious and political, believed in freedom of thought and action, and their conviction brought them into conflict with the government until such time as they had won their "rights." These rights were won concurrently with the establishment of the industrial system, at which stage the revolutionists became the conservatives and enlisted their new powers in the defense of the status quo with as much zeal as they had formerly attacked it.

Thus it is that the great industrialists in England today hold the reins of government, whereas three centuries ago they were mere city aldermen, busying themselves with the petty details of local ordinances; and conversely, the nobility have been relegated to a back seat in national affairs—to a legislative assembly where their power is nominal rather than actual. To put it more concretely, it was an industrialist, the Rt. Hon. Stanley Baldwin of Baldwin & Company (sheet and metal workers) who directed the policy of the Empire, while the peers approved (because they could do nothing else) the legislation prepared by the Commons.

The picture of class in England, however, is not simply a picture of economic assertion on the part of the bourgeoisie. The social structure did not immediately collapse with the economic landslide from the medieval town economy. Men might become rich within their life span, but they did not thereby become noble. For generations, to the contrary, certain sources of wealth were socially detrimental. Large profits merely served to emphasize a nonaristocratic origin. And this aristocratic tradition still has a powerful, though less apparent, influence in English society today. The newly rich pickle manufacturer has not necessarily climbed a rung on the social ladder. The medieval social order is something the student of class must still take into account in his analysis of the modern system.

It is very important, when speaking of a class struggle, to remember that dissatisfaction and resentment began not with the proletariat, who became class-conscious and articulate long after the new economic divisions of society had been in effect, but with the middle classes, who were still not satisfied with the attainment of their economic and political "rights." They wanted social recognition as well. The early nineteenth century bourgeois novelists express with considerable bitterness the resentment felt by their class toward their social superiors. From this resentment sprang snobbishness, an entirely modern and still unmistakably English characteristic.

Nowadays by snobbishness one is inclined to imply disdain on the part of certain individuals toward those they consider their social inferiors. It is well to remember, however, that it began by being the other way round—a feeling of inferiority on the part of the *nouveau riche* in their relationship with the established gentry. Moreover, no matter how disguised modern snobbishness may be, it is still a subconscious resentment of social superiority, a resentment which is inverted by way of compensation. This inversion is apparent in the excessive self-consciousness of the British middle class, and the absence of it among the lower and upper classes, either toward themselves or toward each other.

In medieval times there was no escaping the station in life to which it had pleased God to call a man. His occupation, as his harvest, was remotely and absolutely determined, no more to be changed than the position of hills and rivers. Here was no cause for resentment and hostility. The yeoman, the squire, the lord of the manor, and the king had likewise been ordained by some absolute power to fulfill their particular function. There could be no reasonable grounds for discontent in this concept of society. If there were revolts and dissatisfaction, as there were in the peasant wars which swept through Europe, it was due as much to acts of God as to any fault in the social scheme. Men could not starve to death without protest. So, if it had not been for the crop failures and the plagues, the feudal system might have withstood another millenium of individualistic and liberal propaganda. Socially, as well as economically, it was based on many sound principles of human conduct. Compared to the early industrial periods in Europe, it was even Utopian.

When the township economy was swept away, nothing could have been more definite and sharp than the social distinctions between the three new groups which resulted—the old aristocracy, the new industrialists, and the transformed laboring classes. For a time, there was scarcely any social intercourse at all between them. In Chaucer's days pilgrims on their way to Canterbury had journeyed together without any compunction—the knight, the squire, the parson, the sailor, the cook, and the rest, all traveling along the road without any fuss as to precedence. This absence of class consciousness was impossible, once industrialism, Presbyterianism, and liberalism had spread abroad the doctrine of freedom and individual worth. According to a member of the new middle class, all men were born potentially equal and all were entitled to equal civil rights. What he really meant was that *he* was as good as the next man. By the "nextman" was not implied the mechanic (for obviously the misshapen, inarticulate, unwashed machine-minder could not be so good); but the implication intended was that he, the wealthy, pious, and broad-minded nonconformist, was as good as his so-called social superior. That was the beginning of class consciousness and the beginning of snobbishness. From that moment there could no longer be any social unity in England.

2

New factors and elements are present today to complicate any composite picture of class distinctions in England. Money is one of them, since money can now buy those social attributes which formerly only rank could give—notably manners, good form, and education. Each of these attributes represents basic elements of the British character. Manners are made up of courtesy, grace, self-assurance; good form, of respect for tradition and distrust of reason; education, of the ability to converse in a cultivated accent. Now, these are all attributes which can be acquired. It does not take generations to inculcate courtesy, grace, and self-assurance into an individual who seldom comes into contact with any other type of behavior. Imitation is a factor in human conduct. So with attitude, conversation, and accent: these are all easily acquired characteristics. And in proportion as they are easily acquired, so are they leveling factors in the social conformation. They will give the merchant's or the miner's son the same outward gloss as the duke's. Anyone who has studied at Oxford, or even visited there, will know this to be true. In the absence of a laboratory test to differentiate blue from ordinary red blood, all that one can tell is what one sees and hears: namely, a number of young men all clad in brown coats and gray trousers, who conduct themselves in the same supercilious and indolent manner, discuss the same gossip, and use a similar local dialect. Where are class distinctions here? They have been superficially lost in the leveling process which privilege calls education.

From this it will be seen that there is another force at work tending to blur the original class distinctions— the force of democratic education. We should be cautious, however, in estimating the influence of democracy in England. There has long been some political democracy, but there has never been a social democracy comparable with that of America, for instance. Education, which in the latter country exerts a leveling influence, accentuates social differences in England. The lower classes, for instance, receive just enough education to make them self-conscious in the presence of the middle classes, who have received enough to make them smug in the presence of everybody. And one of the prime reasons for this—a reason which cannot be too strongly emphasized—is accent.

Accent, I would say, is the most important, the most unequivocable index to class in England. It parallels almost exactly the main socio-economic divisions of society. A workingman almost invariably has a definitely proletarian accent, which, by false philological standards, is held to be linguistically inferior. At the other extreme, the upper classes, which will include the higher professions, use a particular accent which is not necessarily Standard English because it happens to sound like the distant bleating of a goat. In any case, there is no Official Standard English, so that the question does not arise as to the philological excellence of this upper-class accent. In between the extremes of Cockney, on the one hand, and Super-Oxonian on the other, we have a whole gamut of accents corresponding to the infinite gradations of class. If the foreigner is to understand class in England, he must be a trained philologist.

"It is impossible," remarked Bernard Shaw, "for one Englishman to talk to another without either hating his companion or despising him." This comment, although something of an understatement, nonetheless indicates the correlation between class and accent; for since an Englishman's accent reflects so accurately his class, status, education, and probable point of view, the compatriot can divine immediately whether his own social qualifications are better or not so good. The knowledge will supply grounds for resentment or contempt.

There are several more or less objective criteria which can be used as indications of class. Personal appearance, clothes, conversation, living standards, interests, and attitudes will conform to general rules of environment and so indicate roughly social standing. The shrewd observer can pick out a member of the lower classes even in his "Sunday" clothes. He will give himself away by some allegedly vulgar touch, probably by the tightness of his collar. Likewise conversation will be determined by home environment, degree of education, and general experience. Upper-class conversation tends to facetious-ness; middle-class, to pompousness; lower-class, to profanity. It is not to be expected that the workingman will have the style, vocabulary, and range of the higher civil servant. His living standards will be correspondingly inferior; his intellectual interests and attitudes, similarly limited. So that, while there will be increasingly numerous exceptions, these several factors will, on the whole, reflect fairly objectively class distinctions.

3

From what I have said, the reader will conclude that, in spite of the disruption of the old social order and the leveling influences of the new, class distinctions are still fairly sharp in modern England. And this is indeed the case. Moreover, not only are class distinctions everpresent; they are increasingly apparent. As soon as an Englishman gets away from his particular social group, he is aware that he does not belong. This, no doubt, is a purely emotional reaction and not all the evidence in the world can prove or disprove the assertion. It is something that is to be felt rather than measured. Sometimes, however, it can be observed. The arrogance of the upstart toward his economic dependents or the humility of the aristocrat in the presence of his social inferiors are both examples of this class consciousness. Further, the constant efforts of the middle class to impress everyone with their social worth are symptomatic of an inadmissible feeling of inferiority.

All this will have considerable interest for the political scientist. He will want to know to what extent the existence of class distinctions and class consciousness is precipitating a class conflict in England; and then, to what extent the danger of some social revolt is imminent. My answer would be, to a very small extent, because of a number of offsetting factors. On the one hand, social unrest is inevitably provoked by undeniable economic hardships, which have been strong and continuous enough in England to weld the whole of the working class together in organized opposition to exploitation. The Trade Union movement is the material proof of this. The conflict here is entirely an economic one. It can be regarded as two brute forces—one of labor and one of finance—pressing against each other to determine the direction both shall go. It is not altogether accurate, therefore, to speak of economic conflict as a *class* struggle. The whole mass of the workers of England cannot be called one class and the capitalists another. The Marxian concept is too simple for an explanation of English society. From the point of view of *class*, many of the small capitalists and employers belong in the lower brackets; that is, in their mode of life, in their attitudes, habits, amusements, and the like, they belong with the workers; yet in the economic system, their interests are identifiable with those of the upper and middle classes, the landowners and the industrialists.

Hence, the absence of a complete class identity diffuses the force of a class struggle. This is one important factor in the maintenance of the status quo. Another is the philanthropic or reform policy which has determined English legislation for a century or more. In realistic terms, this amounts to making concessions whenever the economic inequalities become too pronounced for the oppressed groups to tolerate any longer.

Nearly all the reforms put through in British legislation have been tactical retreats on the part of the governing classes. Universal franchise, elementary education, social and health insurance, pensions, have all been of this kind, and most of them have been passed by conservative governments. This is the simple secret of Britain's comparative political and social stability, as it is the explanation of the absence of any successful communist movement. The working classes are never oppressed quite enough.

4

These are economic and political factors. There are also social forces which work toward or against social stability. The real class distinctions of education, accent, and attitudes are observable causes of dissatisfaction and emotional unrest. The lower classes are frequently made aware of their intellectual inferiority. This may seem vague on paper, but it is bitter enough in reality. For the sensitive person realizes that he is missing part of the fun, that he is not so well equipped for the battle of life. And these differences in attainments reflect corresponding inequalities in opportunity, separating a class from the group immediately above it —the lower class from the lower middle class; this from the middle class proper. It can be seen in a study of the relationships existing between the adjacent groups—the asserted superiority of the petty shopkeepers' children to the ragamuffins of the artisans; while these, for their part, make life as unpleasant as possible for better dressed and better educated children. But here again, the characteristically English policy of reform minimizes the danger of revolt by minimizing the causes of it. Concessions are opportunely made toward better educational opportunities for even the lowest and poorest classes.

The claim that every English adolescent has a reasonable opportunity to "improve" himself is quite accurate. The elementary schools are good, particularly in their care of the children's health; and arrangements are made for adolescents to continue their studies when they leave school at the age of fourteen. They have their night schools, or "evening classes" as they are called. Further, a liberal provision of scholarships starts the feet of many children of the lower classes on the rungs of the social ladder. They gain entry to secondary schools, go on to universities, marry better class women, and become within the course of a generation members of the middle class. This process is continuous, giving solidity as well as stolidity to an increasingly conservative and respectable society. Anyone who has visited England recently will see ample evidence of this leveling process. Vast areas are being covered by small suburban houses, each belonging to the family which lives in it— a condition tending to induce a sense of social well-being and satisfaction.

Thus it is that, in spite of the sharp distinctions and the several factors which make those distinctions intolerable, the English governmental and private tradition tends to obfuscate the real issue, so that the class struggle is really a struggle for existence (a decent one) rather than a hostility toward some other social group. The communists, therefore, in depicting the capitalists as corpulent, frock-coated bankers grasping huge money bags, are exorcising a nonexistent devil, as far as the English are concerned; and in stressing the class struggle and the common good of the workers, they overlook the actual indifference, apart from the common need for good wages, short hours, and some degree of social security, which one workingman feels for another. In more philosophical terms, one might say that class unity is felt more in an antagonism toward another group—and generally toward the group immediately above one's own—than a compelling need of *esprit de corps*. The English workingman is not proud of his class. He does not live by or for it. Rather, he strives to better *himself*, which from his point of view means to obtain an easier and less menial job, a better home to live in, good clothes, and education for his children. What percentage of the English realize this desire it is impossible to say; but as long as a shrewd government adopts a reform platform, their sympathies are definitely not with a revolutionary movement.

Thus England, as far as its class system is concerned, is still quasi-feudal in its system, although it has all the presumed advantages and all the obvious shibboleths of democracy as well. It is possible, however, that its strength comes from the former rather than the latter, from the vestiges of absolutism it retains rather than from the forms of democracy it affects.

VII

Education

NOTHING could show more clearly the positiveness of English class distinctions than the English system of education; and nothing, perhaps, could differentiate more appositely the American from the British brand of democracy than their respective attitudes toward education. The American historians tell us that the schoolhouse was set up side by side with the blockhouse on the American frontiers. The schoolteacher, instead of the missionary as in the British Empire, followed the explorer; the textbook, instead of the bottle, came behind the rifle.

Even if we discount some of the delightful optimism with which the official American historians view the cause of democracy on their continent, there is no gainsaying the bigness, lavishness, and enthusiasm of the American school system, a truly democratic system. England is correspondingly niggardly, correspondingly aristocratic in its approach. The English are sometimes inclined to pride themselves on this aristocratic or se-

lective point of view. They march up Oxford and Cambridge to defend their arguments, and amuse themselves
taking a tilt at American degrees in cooking, first aid
to the injured, and drugstore practice. What, they ask
—and with considerable justice—is the value of a
thesis on the five methods of dishwashing? Why a doctor's degree for the "Frying of Doughnuts in Butter
Fat"? If in butter, why not in lard? If in lard, why not
in margarine? and so forth. This, say the English, is not
education or scholarship, but busy work with no other
significance than the annoying letters (A.B., M.S.,
neither of which means anything to the Englishman,
unless he interprets the latter as Master of Sewing)
which the graduates of American universities like to
append to their names.

Although there is, indeed, something a bit outlandish
about an educational system which awards degrees to
students who are adept at counting noses, a system
which tends to substitute calculating machines for reflective thinking, it might well be contended that the
English method of emphasizing Latin prosody in an
age of television and the quantum theory is itself a bit
inadequate. What the English omit to take into consideration is the fact that their educational theory has
simply not evolved with the times. A few modifications
have been made in the actual system, compulsory education being one of them; but so far as the objectives
are concerned, there has been no change, no adaptation
of purpose to function. For while English education is
still aristocratic or humanist in nature and content, the
needs of the growing democracy are popular and scientific; and while the nation purports to be a democracy, it

continues in its scholarship the imperialistic traditions. An examination of the next English public school boy the reader meets will clarify these statements. The English public school boy is the result of a nonfunctional, nondemocratic education at its worst. In consequence, behold a little monster who pens Latin hexameters with ludicrous skill, and regards all who did not attend Eton or Harrow as lesser breeds without the law.

Those English who did not attend the three or four schools and universities with international reputations based as much on their ivy-clad walls as on their scholarship, may be regarded as having had no formal education at all. This is a fearful deficiency to have to admit in a country of universal college graduates like America; therefore, most Englishmen dissemble a little about their education at home. Those of us who have received no education because we did not attend Oxford (Cambridge for some mysterious reason being unheard of in this country) must admit the justice of the inquirer's loss of interest on learning the fact. We are grateful, indeed, that he does not press us into admitting a horrible relationship with provincial universities such as those of London, Birmingham, Bristol, and the rest. If he does, what pangs of shame we feel as we answer brightly, "London" or "Leeds." Sometimes we can get by with London. It sounds vaguely large and important. But if queries are raised as to its age, London is lost. The university is not even a hundred years old.

One's lack of education—and we are speaking of the real thing, the ripe, eight-hundred-year-old vintage—is a constant source of embarrassment to Englishmen abroad. Sometimes we are talked into asserting we have attended Oxford. There is no escaping the appeal of college undergraduates and provincial newspaper reporters. If we appear on a lecture platform, we have to be something more than the "well-known English lecturer and writer." We have to be "Mr. Fitzsimmons of Oxford University, England. . . . " Then terrified at the enormity of the sacrilege, we burn our boats and admit we attended Balliol, that being the only college whose name we are sure of. Or perhaps we can make a feeble joke on the spelling versus the pronunciation of *Magdalen*. The situation is sometimes saved by a bold spirit sidetracking his pursuers into a reference to Caius (pronounced "keys") College, Cambridge. One's education is then forgotten in considerations of the drollness of English pronunciation.

But what horror the well-known English lecturer and writer experiences when, having admitted that he is an Oxford graduate, he is asked to address an American audience on education in England! He knows by now that education in England can only mean education at Oxford. He must talk, therefore, about Oxford. He searches his memory for facts and stories about this legendary place. Isn't there some regulation about bowling hoops down the High Street? It's called the *High*, that's right. And didn't the Balliolian (or whatever these Superior Persons call themselves), with whom he was once privileged to chat, say something about getting in by ten o'clock and "bulldogs" and pub crawling? It's all very vague, but possibly the well-known lecturer has time to look up a back number of *The Reader's Digest*. *The Reader's Digest* being infallibly encyclopaedic, he finds an article, sure enough, by a

Rhodes scholar. It is the very thing—full of anecdotes about proctors and bullers, porters and their wives, halls and Latin graces. The lecturer renders it with grace and charm, and many a sly witticism at the expense of those American degrees in cooking and drugstore practice. At Oxford they prepare gentlemen and higher civil servants; in an American university, only footballers. At Oxford they inculcate a profound skepticism into youth; in America, only a shallow optimism. At Oxford, whatever a man does (follow stories about pub crawling and pursuits by proctors), he will not deliberately tell a lie. To illustrate. A Magdalen man was once hauled before his don (is it don or rector or what?) for a misdemeanor. "Who was that notorious woman you were seen with last night, Mr. Pycraft?" "That, sir? Oh, that was my sister!" "But, sir, the woman is a notorious strumpet!" "I know, sir. Mother and I worry about her constantly."

There is not much of a laugh. The Englishman is not perturbed, though, and finishes off his rehash of the *Digest* in fine style. Very successful, he concludes, as elderly ladies press round to inform him of the interesting fact that their great-uncles came from Yorkshire. Very successful, very gratifying—until the president of the college shakes his hand and remarks drily, "Very nice, Dr. Fitzsimmons. I've read it before somewhere."

2

The American reader will find it difficult to envisage a state in which some 95 per cent of the population receive no formal education at all. Other foreigners, too, who are positive that the English are unhuman be-

cause of too perfect an upbringing, will be astonished at
this state of affairs. All will require a fuller explanation.

It depends on the definition of "formal education,"
and this definition has been intimated in the references
to the English public schools and two venerable universities. It is true that 95 per cent of the population,
which have not attended an exclusive public school or
an expensive university, have had schooling; but they
have not, in the English sense, acquired an education.
For the primary emphasis in the English system is not
upon producing a well-informed general public, but in
producing an elegant sufficiency of well-behaved civil
servants—men, and to a limited extent women, who
can speak in a certain superior manner, dress with that
passionless formality which so impresses the outside
world, and generally conduct themselves with that
formidable aloofness which, together with boiled shirts,
upholds the Empire in the most remote corners of the
earth. These attitudes of speech, dress, and manner explain the purposive impracticality of English education.

To the American it may appear as if the end of English education as promulgated in the "best" institutions
is to make the individual who receives it as unsuitable
as possible for the so-called "battle of life." This easy
conclusion takes no account of that infallible British
practicality which underlies all their achievements and
actions. Their education, in spite of its concern with
Greek epigrams and Latin odes, in spite of its obsession
with abstractions and indifference to practice, is the
most pragmatic in the world: it is a deliberate preparation of a chosen few for specific careers by encasing them
in an intellectual armor impervious to any new or queer

ideas. The Englishman who has had the benefit of seven years' grounding in the classics is so hardened mentally that he will never question anything again nor ever have the slightest uncertainty as to the rightness of his own conduct and the system of which he finds himself a custodian. It is this fact which has made foreign critics justly remark that, while Englishmen in the course of the centuries have been known to die of bullet wounds, not a single one of them has ever been slain by an idea. For this they may thank their education.

The foreign observer will want a fuller explanation of these statements. Let him examine the several stages of English education in the persons of the privileged few who receive it. Let him examine *in situ*, if possible, the public schools and public school boys, remembering that the *real* public schools are private, and that the really public schools are of no account in the English educational system.

The public school proper, in its role of private institution, is based upon the most rigorously conservative standards of social merit. Where birth is lacking, the candidate must be able to compensate with irrefutable wealth. The major reward of attending a public school is the firm assurance, which never leaves the alumnus afterward, that Etonians or Harrovians, as the case may be, are the cream of society and all the rest, the skimmed milk; or, as the public school boy would say, there are his people and "cads." This simple and useful classification of humanity into two parts is indispensable in later life, in the executive and administrative posts for which public school boys are destined. Hence, in their dealings with subordinates and foreigners and all the lesser breeds without the law, these model Englishmen, now physically adult civil servants, have the unshakable conviction of intrinsic superiority. Obviously such a conviction together with a complete imperviousness to ideas makes them inviolate and invincible.

The next advantage the chosen few receive from their public school is the satisfaction of accepting or enforcing a system of organized cruelty which effectively atrophies any emotion or humanity the newcomer may have brought with him. It is generally supposed abroad that the English are devoid of ordinary feelings; but this generalization is only true of the public school boys who have had their feelings kicked or tormented or bullied out of them. In earlier times, when the British Empire needed sterner stuff than it apparently needs today, the masters helped in this process of dehumanization. Like the redoubtable Hunter of whom Boswell reports that, while he flogged his pupils (including the ponderous Doctor) unmercifully, he was wont to say, "And this I do to save you from the gallows," those ferocious headmasters—Parker, Arnold, Squeers—wielded a stick with a strong and morally righteous right arm. What the masters left incomplete, the prefects finished off with the joyous cooperation of the bullies; so that all small boys were effectively sore and miserable and suppressed, until their turn came to hand on the lofty tradition of blows and kicks and sneers.

"Impossible!" we exclaim in these new days of child emancipation; or "Exaggerated!"

Not at all. We who attended a private "public" school have our memories—something else for the English to suppress according to the dictates of loyalty. But even if we do not tell, we remember those first days at school, the departure of our mothers, the feeling of desolation, the trembling lip, the comfort of tears. Then the jibes and the humiliations and the bewilderment, joyously interpreted by the "big boys" as native stupidity—and punished accordingly. Looking back, it is strange and bitter that we were hurt because we were sick during the day or coughed at night or wet our beds.

It is strange in a supposedly pacifistic country, where suggestions of compulsory military service are met with considerable moral indignation, that we were compelled to march about to the harsh commands of a retired Indian sergeant, chosen, apparently, for his ingrained brutality. We are told at the dear old school reunions what fine fellows the regimen of blows and scanty food made of us. One wonders. Fresh air built up our bodies, long studies our minds. But what happened to our emotions? The frigidity and unhumanity of the educated Englishman is the answer. These characteristics he exploits or foreigners exploit for him, so that his impassivity and submission to forms are considered almost godlike in a world of violence and protest. However, the Englishman, inscrutable behind his mask of good breeding, is continuously uncomfortable and petulant, eager to break through his bonds of correctness and to establish contact with his fellow humans. But if the public school training has been effective, he can never achieve humanity—either with strangers or friends or father, mother, or wife. He is condemned to two score years and ten of gelidity and for the rest to a model senescence, pitifully interspersed with ill-timed attempts at lechery.

3

Those public school boys who are fortunate enough to go on to a university are suddenly given a chance to lead their own life and become comparatively normal— at least, normal underneath the public school veneer, which they can never entirely lose. First of all, they find themselves transferred from a barracks to a monastery. Their masters are no longer officers and drill sergeants, but teachers and even friends. Their comrades are not humiliated privates, identifiable by a number but otherwise all equally craven, but are individuals with variant moods, pleasures, and even ideas. It is an indescribable relief to escape the eternal theme of sex, the sole compensation of the public school existence, to find a number of merry or gentle pleasures which leave no restlessness.

From public school to university is from cage to woodland. The English undergraduate shows this in his very face and manner and conduct. His expression is one of naïve delight; his manner, rather pathetically eager; his actions, impetuous and irresponsible. And all this exuberance is grafted onto that pompous public school boy dignity which maddens the outside world. Hence, the English undergraduate, solemn yet strenuously merry; silent yet definitely opinionated; reserved yet embarrassingly confidential. When sober, he is inclined to intimidate a normal individual; when drunk, to shock. And all of these strangely assorted and tortuous attitudes of his make-up are cast in a sound mold of true scholarship, for he is armed with a precision of language which cuts right through an opponent's clumsy rant; and his opinions are implemented by a thorough reading which gives strength to his most careless witticism. A remarkable, formidable, pathetic youth.

The first thing the university does for the public school boy is to reverse the principles and opinions he brought away with him from Eton or Harrow or Marlborough. His knowledge and appreciation remain unchanged, for they are founded on an uncompromising study of the best in philosophy and art; but his jingoistic conception of the world as belonging in fact or in principle to the British Empire, his unshakable conviction of Etonian superiority, and his firm belief that there is no alternative to the present system, are suddenly and joyously abandoned at the first mention of Karl Marx. For the new world of ethical and economic speculation are as liberating to him as the new world of men who are not drill sergeants, youths who are not privates, and girls who are not purchasable with a quarter's allowance. His wings unfold over these immeasurable spaces and he flies away straight into the fastnesses of atheism, romanticism, and communism. If he doesn't— and there are a few who do not—he no longer has the spirit or the intelligence to appreciate his freedom.

As already pointed out, the authorities are not particularly alarmed by his metamorphosis from a little top-hatted snob to the hatless communist who speaks at street-corner meetings and marches with a column of strikers. For this is a phase they have themselves experienced and outgrown. If the foreign observer were to ask, with surprise or alarm, the fully fledged English conservative, working quietly and steadily in the recesses of Whitehall to maintain British imperialism,

"Why don't you people stop this rabidness of the English students?" the conservative would no doubt reply, "Not at all. They are receiving a very necessary training for suppressing communism where it amounts to something—in India, South Africa, and China. We shall be able to use them for this purpose later on."

Behold, then, the English public school boy and the university student. The former with his limited concepts and unquestioning obedience is destined for small administrative positions in the remoter outposts of the Empire—to him nothing more than a vague generalization for the old school. The drill and punishment he has received will be visited on subject races for the good of the capitalists at home. And the university man, scholarly, liberal, and polished—a little disillusioned and cynical when he reaches maturity; still fond of unorthodox ideas, but only in books—with his mental adroitness, cultivated manners, and double scorn of the masses, he is the perfect statesman. Eton plus Oxford plus Karl Marx have combined to produce that unparalleled phenomenon, the English diplomat.

4

The English public school boys and university men make up not more than 2 or 3 per cent of the population. The others have had schooling, but not education. In English parlance, they have been taught certain mechanical conveniences—how to read the newspaper, write a letter, and count their wages—but they have not been fashioned and polished into gentlemen. A few ambitious or disgruntled spirits are not content with this perfunctory schooling; they are determined to acquire the objective characteristics of the privileged. They go to night schools and learn an atrocious French; they acquire a modicum of physics from a textbook; they struggle through a public library Latin grammar; and they prepare through long nights for the matriculation and higher examinations. Late in the twenties, these pale and hollow-cheeked young men acquire an external B.A., and receive the congratulations and wonder of their friends; but they are no more gentlemen, thereby, than a milkman or a bargee with an honorary degree would be a gentleman. They are not gentlemen in speech or manners or dress or appearance; nor do they get gentlemen's jobs. They do not become higher civil servants or members of parliament or administrators. They teach in elementary and night schools, and write elementary textbooks in their spare time. They are failures because they have not been to Oxford or Cambridge, and every time they drop an aitch or mutate a vowel, they pay a huge indemnity for their temerity and pretensions.

The mass of the population remains schooled but uneducated. They remain likewise human, with exactly the same failings, wants, and aspirations which men suffer from the world over. The foreigner will not be perturbed by their accent or manners or appearance. He will recognize in every bus driver and porter and waitress a human being. There are about forty-five million of them, yet foreigners seldom see them or take them into account in their evaluations of the English. As we have said, most critics are inclined to regard them as some proletarian monster, kept in leash by the acknowledged English gentlemen. It would be truer to say they are kept in servitude by their own ignorance, by the machines they mind, by the material comforts they are doled out in periodical reforms, and by the vast patience of their own natures. For they are born tolerant, good-humored, and amiable. Let us consider them neither monstrous nor menacing, but only profoundly and inalterably human.

VIII

Manners

I

FOR some reason or other, "manners" is a wholesome word like "comely," "buxom," "blithesome," "lusty," "winsome," and all those other simple, pre-Elizabethan words which, in contrast to our modern vocabulary, make no attempt to be artful or specious. Indeed, the fundamental difference between the sixteenth and twentieth centuries might be reduced to a plain difference of vocabulary, with all that the change implies. Thus, "mores" for "manners," "pretty" for "comely," "grazing land" for "green pastures," are very symptomatic of relevant points of view. The difference is quite apparent in the elaborate terminology now necessary to define the elemental sexual relationships. That which in old romances was merely a case of "going in unto" a woman and "lying with" her, is now a matter of two hundred pages preparation, a chapter hinting at the act itself, and the rest of the book explaining the complicated psychological outcome.

As with words, so with attitudes; they have lost their pristine simplicity and directness. There are no longer mere "manners" in England—or in America, for that matter; but "good form" in the former country and "behavior patterns" in the latter.

Once manners made man, which is by no means true of good form. Manners are the whole anatomy of an individual; good form, only his social graces. We do not deal here with the Englishman's whole mode of life, but must confine ourselves to the modern and effete significance of manners, and speak of "good form."

It has often been asserted by foreign observers that good form is the alpha and omega of the English character; or, to put it another way, the armor which protects the Englishman against the assault, the inquiry, or merely the amiability of the outside world: that the national behavior which is strictly determined by canons of good form makes him impregnable. According to some critics, such canons make him inviolate by devitalizing him, and to all outward appearances the well-mannered Englishman is indeed a passionless and inscrutable being. First of all, he vigorously suppresses the emotions which lighten or darken other men's faces: neither anger, sorrow, nor humor crease the fine lines of his countenance—save, and the exception is significant, in the case of the misfortunes of animals. The plight of humanity, whether of his own or some other nationality, leaves the Englishman superficially unmoved; but the sight of cruelty to an animal will metamorphose him into an unexpected demon from whose face flashes the terrible lightning of fury. We may see the Englishman on the continent, walking circumspectly and secretive among the curious glances and strong smells of foreigners, jerk into action if a whip flays the flanks of an overloaded horse.

What, then, are the causes, and what the symptoms, of good form? The puzzled observer is inclined to rush in with the assertion that the English consider themselves so irrefutably superior to the rest of the world that their diffidence is one of contempt. Examples of British jingoism are brought forward to prove this contention. Those imperialistic bullyings of the deity which distinguish Rudyard Kipling's poetry redound with statements of British preeminence, both physical and moral; in fact, the rest of the world is dismissed as "lesser breeds without the law," the law in this case resembling a public school boy's elementary rules of conduct administered by a retired Indian colonel. There is, indeed, an interesting group known as the British Israelites which, contending for the dubious honor of being the Lost Tribe, combine in a characteristically British manner the religion of the Old Testament with the politics of the nineteenth century. According to the British Israelites, the English are the chosen people and, as such, will inherit the earth, a supposition which is proven to their own satisfaction by the "readings of the pyramids."

So it is that the number of self-assertive and aggressive sentiments held by the British, and often patched up by poet laureates for state occasions, strikes the foreign observer as a bland assurance of divine destiny; and thus convinced, we are told, the British indicate the fact to the rest of the world by carrying good manners to the point of offensiveness. The natural curiosity and bonhomie of other men they meet with polite but frigid negation. They are startled even when their favorite topic of the weather is introduced by a stranger—not startled in any harelike manner, however; but alarmed into a hardening of the mask which they present to the world in lieu of a face. A bus has a minor collision in Paris, for instance. The French occupants scream; the Germans analyze the situation; the Americans grin. The English only stiffen, until the others become aware from the atmosphere that the whole proceedings—the cries, the curiosity, the amusement—are somehow in very bad taste—the collision itself, the excitement of the crowd, and the diverse emotions of those concerned.

But whereas the chilly phenomenon of English good form is indisputable, the causes of it are not so simple and banal as the foreigner is inclined to suppose. The usual explanation of British priggishness is really only an involuntary compliment on the part of those who advance it. A more accurate and first-hand knowledge of the English will suggest entirely different reasons—reasons of vague discomfort and a definite feeling of inferiority. The discomfort springs from an awareness of their own natures; the inferiority from their emotional limitations. The Englishman, too, wants to laugh or cry, as the occasion warrants; but his upbringing and traditions and the presence of his compatriots restrain him. He sees no intrinsic virtue in woodenness. Why should he? It is more becoming and more amusing to be alive; or, as the English say, to be *natural*, by which they mean, to be *human*. But let it be remembered that three centuries of Puritanism militate against any overt manifestations of humanity.

The English, to their lasting regret, accepted unconditionally the doctrine of original sin; and being an unimaginative as well as an earnest people, thorough as well as honest, they did not shirk the full implications of divine indignation. From the most merry people in Europe, they became in the course of several generations the most melancholy; from a "nest of singing birds," a nation of hymn singers; and from a race of jolly blasphemers, a people who "worshipped God for spite." This was not their fault; it was their loyalty.

The English, though accused of being the most ruthless people on earth on the inconclusive evidence of their military conquests, are really the most docile; and far from being the most obstinate, they are the most tractable. But unfortunately for their peace of mind, they have overdeveloped consciences and a strong sense of practical justice. These attributes, together with their industry, make them rulers of one-third of the world. Yet there is no satisfaction in it for them any more than there is satisfaction in being virtuous without the opportunities for vice. Hence, the English rationalize their conduct and their "good form" in terms of duty—and, for their pains, are accused of being hypocrites. They are neither hypocritical nor smug; they are merely conscientious. Seeing such unnecessary conscientiousness with such unbounded prosperity, foreign cynics direct their clever jibes at the English. Bewildered and wounded, the English take refuge in stolidity. Their good form is a convenient cloak, particularly where the body beneath is hypersensitive.

2

It is really very strange that the English, who have contributed so much in their literature to the gaiety of nations, should be suspected of such unmitigated melancholy. Indeed, one of their own doctors termed hypochondria the Englishmen's disease. Yet for large humor, huge laughter, deep potations, and general roister-doisterousness, English literature is unexcelled; so much so, that Shakespeare, Jonson, and Fielding are accused by French critics of being uncouth, or we might say, *too* human. At all events, such literature lacks the good form which the English manifest excessively in their actual lives. It is as though in literature they prefer a deep, jovian laughter; in life, a drawing-room smirk.

We might mildly suggest that Sir John Falstaff and Parson Adams and Mr. Sam Weller were as good Englishmen as any who were born of women; only Sir John never got much farther than the Garter Inn and Sam Weller, as a true Cockney, never much beyond Epping Forest. But these jolly Englishmen once enlivened England, and still do for those who know where to look for them.

If only foreign critics would go once to the Derby instead of twice to Ascot! If only they could roast chestnuts round a Yorkshire fireplace at Christmas instead of spending so much time in the Strand Palace Hotel in the summer! If only they got themselves wedged in a third-class railway carriage on a Bank Holiday instead of motoring through the Shires in the middle of the week! Then they would see some of the twenty million Englishmen who have no more regard for good form than they have for the lost continent of Atlantis—the Cockneys, costermongers, railwaymen, stevedores, miners—all of them pretty grimy, reasonably ugly (except for the girls between the ages of seventeen and twenty-three), and so exclusively human that they are blind to anything but their fellow humans. From this great reservoir of humble people spring those wells of geniality and humor which have watered the best English literature from the time of the Anglo-Saxon Riddles. The foreigner who wishes to discover the fountainhead of those waters and the observer who is unwilling to accept without some investigation the belief that all the English are stiff-necked, should take into account the common people, who have at least escaped the bondage of good form, even while they have been economically enslaved.

For a long time cleanliness was considered the virtue next in importance to godliness. A clean shirt was next to hymn singing in the hierarchy of English morality. In fact, without the clean shirt the hymn singing was impossible, ingress to any decent place of worship being barred to anyone without it. Hence, righteous churchgoers always visited the house of God in their most uncomfortable finery, many of them adding to their chance of salvation by having a bath the night before. But the workingman had no place in this strictly economic interpretation of sanctity. He had neither bath nor Sunday clothes. He could not, then, go to church and mix with decent people. It follows that he could not attain godliness.

This was really very fortunate so far as the national resources for geniality and jolliness were concerned, for apart from the working classes, the rest of society was being so strenuously godly and clean that there was little opportunity for fun or laughter. Victoria's remark on an awful occasion will be remembered, when that imprudent courtier who attempted to produce a smile on the royal countenance was rebuffed with a frigid, "We are not amused." The English upper and middle classes are still "not amused" by the ordinary comicalities of existence. Their good form holds the lash above their sense of humor. Good form has made even laughter polite, so that Gargantua, the Wife of Bath, Sir John Falstaff, and all that jolly company of gourmands and guzzlers and idolaters would be as grotesque in the best English society as a Tartar who had been on horseback for a week.

Not so with the lower classes, however. They have their own mighty quaffers, their own inexhaustible gossips, their own fat, round men as impressive as any in books; and that is why every seeker after the old English jollity—the observer who is not content with the hypothesis that the English are unhuman—must mingle with the crowd, travel in cheap conveyances, rub shoulders in the four-ale bars of public houses, visit the places frequented by the lower five, and patronize their amusements. What enlightenment and what jollity await the adventurous foreigner who foregoes the usual procedure of staring at crumbling castles and mossy mansions to slip silently off in the direction opposite to that indicated in the guidebook!

If he goes with the conducted tour, he will see a historical England, and be inevitably disillusioned in consequence. If he goes with the tour, he will see the conventional English, and be definitely ill at ease as a result. But if he disappears into the fastnesses of London or sets out from Plymouth with a knapsack on his back, he will have a good chance of discovering the English, while learning something about their real manners as well. He may even stumble across their "secret": that their good form is largely a mark to hide an uncomfortable feeling of being so very English and of possibly not belonging to the rest of humanity. But good form is not universal among them. The "other half" live without it—live boisterously, jollily, not giving a damn for the Empire, good form, Moody and Sankey's collected hymns, or the clean shirt which is so near to godliness. It would be just as true to say, therefore, that if half of the English live their lives according to precepts of good form, the other half live them without any precepts whatsoever. And this is a very comforting thought for those of us English who would rather be human than exemplary.

IX

Attitudes

I

JUST as it is true that the English, as Bernard Shaw has pointed out, have never lost a battle fairly, so it is true that they are never wrong without good cause; or, as one of the national sentiments has it, an Englishman wrong is safer than a Frenchman right.

This being the case, we must expect to find the English pretty categorical in their beliefs and attitudes. The conviction of certainty is apparent enough in some instances. Britons never, never, never will be slaves. We don't want to fight, but by Jingo if we do . . . we'll fight and we'll conquer again and again. There is more than a calm assurance here. There is a clenching of the teeth and a thrusting out of the jaw, an expression which is nowadays being outscowled in other quarters. But it is only occasionally that England shows her might, or, as the patriotic cartoonists depict it, that the lion raises his majestic (and somewhat moth-eaten) head. For one thing, the indubitable interest of the divine being in the British Empire gives a feeling of strength, in addition to that provided by the navy. A somewhat patriarchal God is monopolized as the "Lord of our far-flung battle line." One sometimes wonders what would be the attitude of the British toward Jehovah if He failed to recognize the righteousness of their cause. So far He has not failed; to the contrary, from the earliest times He could be relied upon to turn up just in time to save the last battle—and the British Empire.

One sometimes wonders, too, whether the English do not overwork their Supreme Bailiff with demands to water their farmlands, fight their battles, keep them safe from harm, and then take time out to steer a ship across the English channel in the manner described by their poet, Joseph Harris:

> The Winds, and Waves, and Flowing Tide,
> Did Espouse and Battle on our Side;
> Th' Almighty's Steady, Pow'rful Hand,
> Held the Rudder, till the Bark did Land.

But the English are hard workers themselves, and they expect industriousness from their God.

Whether it be some inner strength of the English or simply a lack of imagination, it is certainly true that they settle all problems presented by religion, morality, politics, art, and the rest with a complete disregard for emotion. In religion God as the Chief Bailiff of the Empire is propitiated with a high military rank for his undeniable services. Public relations are conducted along the convenient business lines of making honesty the best policy, a very neat compromise between altruism and cupidity. In politics a most practical compromise is reached between the voice of the people and the answer of Civil Service. Where the American system must carry the burden of bribery and corruption, the English carries only the weight of parliamentary oratory; and where other nations attempt to improve conditions by occasionally decimating a section of the population, the English stage a parade in Hyde Park in order to enjoy all the pleasures of being suppressed in a good cause with no other injuries than those of being whacked on the shins by a policeman's truncheon.

The difficult and thorny problem of art the English have solved by divorcing it from all normal life. Art, like the morality of artists, is excused on the grounds of eccentricity; for the English are a sensible as well as a tolerant people, and realize, where the matter is hopeless, that further pressure is useless. Art and artists, therefore, are ignored on the grounds that indifference and hunger are the best curbs upon nonconformity.

While it is true that the English have produced some of the most facile and provocative thinkers in the history of the world, it is likewise true that, as a nation, they are not an argumentative or a thinking people. *argumentative* Once again the difference between the remarkable few and the mediocre many should be emphasized in order to avoid false conclusions. Above all, let it be understood that, should an Englishman be heard to express striking or original thoughts, he will in all probability be a genius or highly talented person, who would be somewhat suspect in the best English society. For English manners and English attitudes do not permit of novel ideas. These are too startling, and therefore impolite. True, iconoclasms and witticisms which may look for the moment like real ideas are tossed about by the upper middle classes back and forth across a well-plenished dinner table; but these are all confined to superficialities and generalities, which is no doubt as it should be over chicken and Veuve Clicquot. But no respectable member of the middle class will ever be heard expressing an idea outside the pale of polite acceptance, unless he is callously indifferent to the feelings of the company. As for the lower classes, they have no ideas, only wants.

This mental hiatus is sturdily bridged, however, by very definite opinions, hard-set impressions, unshakable convictions. Herein lies one of the secrets of Britain's material success. The Empire has been built on opinions, not ideas. Commercial success is based on an attitude, not a philosophy. If ideas had any influence with the English, India would be self-governing and America a part of the British Empire. Nay, the country itself might still be part of the continent, as it was intellectually in medieval times. But all this is speculation against the inalterable logic of being right, and the English are always right, especially as they have the might to prove it.

They evince this trait in their attitudes toward alien peoples. They have no knowledge and very few ideas about other nationalities. They are genuinely incredulous upon seeing a Frenchman without a beard or a German with one. The former has to have gesticulating hands, the latter a square head, because that is the traditional impression. They have always been a little amazed that other men look as they look, walk on two legs, ride horses, get married, and make homes. They prefer to stress the differences between others and themselves, rather than the similarities. Any slight variations in clothes please them immensely. Strange languages confirm their impression of basic strangeness, and all the stories of foreign monstrosities and aberrations give them considerable mental satisfaction.

One might illustrate this by reference to their impressions of the Americans, whom they have the greatest difficulty in accepting because of the various superficial resemblances to themselves. They seize, therefore, upon the grotesque aspects of American life and character. If the average Englishman were suddenly asked to play the role of an American, he would immediately screw up his nose, request a pair of horn-rimmed spectacles, and remark in an emasculated voice, "Say, Bo, you ain't seen nothink yet." If he were pressed to continue the part, he would no doubt intensify his facial grimace and explain, "Say, Bo, are you telling me? Yes, suh;" after which there might be a reference to "lil ole New York" and various cant phrases current in the United States a decade or so ago.

The English attitude toward America is, and always has been, based on the impression that the Americans are deliberately obnoxious. Englishmen would interpret in this light the behavior and voices of Americans, their appearance, their clothes, their speech, their weather, and not omit the hundred-and-one petty offenses of gum chewing, expectorating, and sight-seeing in droves. When the English read in their newspapers, as they are reading all the time, that the gangsters are again active in Chicago or some unprecedented casualty has occurred, a terrific flood or a gruesome train accident, they remark almost philosophically, "Well, that's America"; with a definite implication, mind you, that, while it has been expressly engineered to hurt the English people's sensibilities, it hasn't succeeded, because they expected it. Moreover, they regard American men as too virile (or assertive, they would say) and American women as too well groomed. The chief American crime, say the English, is that they talk too much— American loquacity being interpreted as bad form; their linguistic resourcefulness, as sheer bombast.

It is sometimes supposed that this is due in part to the failure of the English to revise their attitudes toward the Americans from the time of the Revolution. Let it be definitely understood, however, that the English are not smarting under the stigma of military defeat. The English, after all, have never been beaten *fairly*. Someone must have cheated somewhere—and there are valid grounds for accepting this bland excuse. It is not the defeat, then, but the simple inability to comprehend how a nation could repudiate the English system. The Islanders take it as a personal affront that a people not a hundred years old should thumb their noses, as it were, at the ponderous and complicated English regime. The psychology is exactly that of a conservative parent who cannot understand why his offspring should want to be so different from and independent of his father. To the parent the rebellious son will always appear an upstart; and that is how the American people strike the English.

This is very apparent in the matter of American speech. Nothing gives the English more exquisite satisfaction than the (to them) monstrosities of American dialectic variations. In the next chapter we are to analyze in more detail the nature and significance of the English language; but we may as well note here the importance of the English attitude in this particular matter. This attitude ranges from sheer horror to supercilious amusement, from righteous indignation to a kind of pained surprise. Certain nineteenth century critics ascribed the alleged deficiencies of American speech to deficiencies of the national character. The Very Reverend Henry Alford, D. D., dean of Canterbury, was one such critic who routed out the moral element in his "Plea for the Queen's English." "Look," he exclaims, "at the process of deterioration which our Queen's English has undergone at the hands of the Americans. Look at those phrases which so amuse us in their speeches and books; at their reckless exaggerations and contempt for congruity; and then compare the character and history of the nation—its blunted sense of moral obligation and duty to man." Much the same protest is still being voiced with similar reasons even today.

"I cannot refrain," reports the Chief Constable of Wallasey, "from commenting adversely on the pernicious and growing habit of . . . youths to use Americanisms, with nasal accompaniment, in order to appear, in their own vernacular, *tough guys.*"

All good Englishmen, on hearing of a habit so pernicious as using "foreign" words, could easily explain, to their own satisfaction, the prevalence of crime in Wallasey. Crime and Americanisms would forever after in their minds have a causal relationship.

2

The English regard America as an indefinitely large territory inhabited by people with nasal voices and horn-rimmed spectacles. Some of these inhabitants, the "cuties," are pleasant to look upon, but so utterly incomprehensible in their speech that they would not make attractive companions for long. All these Americans have lots of money and lots of "pep," both of which possessions account for their numerousness and noisiness in Europe, where they are attempting to buy up all the old castles and relics and traditions which they so lamentably lack themselves. For, according to English opinion, these unfortunate people have no history and no culture, and are, in their hearts, distressed by the deficiency. They compensate, therefore, by a cynical and disrespectful manner even in the sacrosanct presence of institutions and customs hundreds of years old.

From this point, the English people's knowledge of America gets increasingly vague. They have heard of New York, Chicago, San Francisco, and Hollywood. They know that America abounds in universities, but that only one of them is ancient enough to take knowledge seriously; namely, Harvard, with the accent on the second syllable. All the other schools are presumably filled with people known as "co-eds," blondified specimens of which bore them in American films. They only know, in brief, that America is in some way a strange and romantic country. Secure in their own mediocrity and pedestrianism, many of them think with something like longing of the white skyscrapers of New York, the dark mysteries of Hollywood, and even the long, grassland of the prairie, which they are convinced is still inhabited by Indians with scalps at their waists. "Armed with bows and arrows," reported the *Daily Telegraph* soberly, "the Indians hunted Dillinger in the wilds of Wisconsin." It is characteristic of the English that a place with a name like "Wisconsin" has to be wild. Outlandish names like Nebraska and Arkansas shake them with sudden mirth. Such barbarisms, they say, wiping their eyes, could be tolerated only by a people like the Americans. For, seriously, are they not an insult to the intelligence?

3

Yet it is possible that the English are themselves a strange people, compounded as they are of so much individual brilliance and so much national mediocrity; of so much narrow insularism and so much practical *weltanschauung;* and of so many prejudices and so much tolerance. It might be argued that this tolerance which distinguishes them from all other peoples springs from their innate sense of superiority. For if constant reiteration of national excellence is any indication, the English regard themselves without any compunction in the matter as the foremost in the world. In addition to the more grandiose sentiments to the effect that "God who made thee mighty" will "make thee mightier yet," there are daily assertions of a more prosaic kind along the lines of "the best in the world." An examination of any daily newspaper will yield a "best in the world" statement. "English-women," announces the *Sunday Express* of June 9, 1929, "are the greatest wonder of the world." "Our judicial system," writes a correspondent to the London *Times*, "is admittedly the finest in the world." So, also, the civil service, the post office, the police force, the zoo, the food, the cooking, and actually the weather (see any textbook of English geography) are all the best in the world. And in case these superlative, though justifiable, claims sound immodest, the *Manchester Guardian* informs its readers, "We are the most self-deprecating people on earth."[1]

On the other hand, the English enjoy immensely criticism and even abuse of themselves. It is possible in England to earn a reputation and an income simply by laughing at the inhabitants. Massed in theaters, they roar with delight at each new jibe at the expense of their sensibilities. They take the unkindest cut as an inverse compliment, and often are chary of the lavish praise with which Americans treat them. For we should not overlook the elements of caution and suspicion in the English character, which may, of course, be a contribution of the Scotch, a people considered by the English as not only unhuman but actually unspeakable. At all events, there is a certain reserve which makes the English pretty formidable as table or traveling companions. Tacitus remarked in his time upon the nongregarious nature of the Germanic tribes, who lived in communities only on condition that each family should be divided from the next by a plot of ground. Today the Englishman's home is still his castle and is usually surrounded by a high wall with broken glass strewn along the top.

[1] All these statements are neatly examined by G. J. Renier in his book, *The English: Are They Human?* Williams & Norgate, London, 1931.

If there appears a discrepancy between the bland self-assertion of superiority on the part of the English and their deep suspicion of hyperbole, it is due to the fact that no sudden enthusiasms carry them away as they so easily carry away the Americans. The easiest thing in the world to sell in America, something novel, is the hardest to sell in England. Englishman resist every change with the immense reserves of moral disapproval which are always at their disposal. As far as mechanical devices for relieving human drudgery are concerned, they suspect something unethical. Should the advantages of a vacuum cleaner as against those of beating a carpet on the clothes line be suggested, the observation will be made that all these new-fangled gadgets are detrimental to the stamina of the race. Yet the English continue, as their latest survey indubitably proves, to deteriorate physically. They have, it appears, almost an obsession with the moral benefits of hard work. The devil, says their proverb, will surely find something for idle hands to do.

The Americans, for that matter, have inherited from the Puritan fathers the gospel of work and monotony; but the ethical implications are nowadays of less account. The Americans now work from mental inertia; the English, from moral fervor. Notice in this respect two words of dreadful import among the English: "slacker" and "loafer." A "slacker," more often than not, will be an individual who is physically incapable of the general norm of industriousness; a "loafer," one who is economically dispossessed. No matter; in spite of the growing recognition of economic hardship and in spite of the customary humanitarian sympathy which is extended in lieu of a drastic remedy for the situation, the unemployed are like pariahs in the English community. Silent and drab at the street corners, they add to the overwhelming grayness of the urban scene. One hurries by, as they stand lolling against greasy walls, caps pulled down over their eyes, cigarettes drooping from the corners of the lips. The younger ones with a ghastly sprightliness jolly the factory girls on their way to work. The older ones organize and talk revolution. The senile just sit on park benches, gray symbols of futility.

To understand the English character, the foreign observer must take into account the manners of the people themselves, the nature of their history, and the climatic conditions of their island. Moral righteousness distinguishes their character; an unbroken tradition determines their lives; continual dampness pervades their homes. From these circumstances they have derived their resoluteness, their sense of destiny, and their inveterate melancholy. Yet in proportion as they are morally firm, they are mentally agile. In proportion as their history is violent, they are personally peaceable. And, as their dispositions are morbid, so is their outlook a wholesome one.

They ask no more in their national maturity than that what they have acquired in material and spiritual possessions should be left undisturbed. Against the rock of their convictions beat the constant tides of uncertainty. Their relationship with the outside world is of this kind. Observers other than we will see whether what they have built over the centuries crumbles away to be washed up on some alien shore.

X

Language

I

O F ALL the monopolistic instincts of the English, their possessiveness in the matter of language is the most pronounced. No people has a vaguer idea as to the true nature and function of their speech, yet none is more proud and jealous of it. The majority of English will not admit, for instance, that the Scotch, Irish, Americans, or Australians have any rights in the use of the Anglo-Saxon tongue. They take the attitude that these nations have borrowed a precious heirloom and tend to abuse the privilege. Indeed, in the whole of Great Britain, there is only one man who speaks the language properly, and that is the person who is using it. While he pronounces correctly, the others, in his opinion, lard their speech with affectations or mis-pronunciations. And even while no two Englishmen speak alike, all fiercely cling to some hypothetical Standard English, a standard just positive enough to exclude the dialects of the rest of the English-speaking people.

The reason for this extraordinarily individualistic and confused attitude lies partly in the factor of class-consciousness; and partly in the motley history of the language itself.

At the time when Raleigh was establishing his luckless colonists in Virginia, all men spoke equally well. There was no Standard English, no superiority of one variant to another. There was not even much concern as to precision, either grammatical or orthographical. Raleigh, for instance, spoke like a provincial, with a broad Devonian accent; and Queen Elizabeth's pronunciation resembled in some particulars that of an inhabitant of the American Middle West; her spelling was that of an "uneducated" person. She said and wrote "skaller," where the modern Standard English requires a supercilious "scholar." She said and wrote "bequive" and "prisiner" for "bequeath" and "prisoner," as an examination of her letters will show. Nobody—not even the grammarians—saw anything irregular in either Raleigh's pronunciation or Elizabeth's spelling. The sixteenth century was unencumbered by compulsory education and the resultant little knowledge of a dangerous thing like grammar. For grammar, after all, belongs along with phrenology and astrology, to the bastard sciences.

It has been mentioned elsewhere in this study of the English to what extent their language is determined by their class distinctions. It was said, and it should be repeated, that in order to understand the social system of these people, the foreigner must understand the implications of the various accents. Then, if he wishes to go one step further in the direction of a more objective point of view, he must know something of the history of the language. Those Americans, for instance, who are vaguely aware of the injustice of the assumption that English English is, in some mysterious way, better than their own speech, will do well to tackle the problem from a philological rather than a patriotic point of view.

They might begin, for example, by remembering the absence of official standards for English, comparable to the standards set by several European academies for the language of their particular countries. They might point out that, philologically, the dialect of Texas has as much claim to priority as that of Oxfordshire; that the accent of the Chicago stockyards is as "good" English as that of the House of Lords. To make these assertions is not to argue for an American standard on the grounds that the United States "are now on their own in language as they have long been on their own in business";[1] it is merely to clarify the issue by coming down to the facts of the matter, irrespective of personal or patriotic prejudices. For to speak of the "best" in accents, to pronounce one as preferable to another, is to introduce certain quite inappropriate concepts into one's judgment—certain *ethical* values which have no more to do with speech as speech than they have with botany, zoology, or the other natural sciences.

We may say, indeed, that the misuse of ethical terms and the intrusion of class or race consciousness into language are responsible for the Americans' century-old inferiority about a tongue as much theirs—and therefore to be spoken and developed according to their

[1] MENCKEN, H. L., editorial, *American Mercury*, January, 1930.

particular needs and wishes—as England's. This inferiority is one of the most obvious complexes evinced by Americans in the presence of the English. One finds Americans becoming almost inarticulate in the hearing of an Englishman—in the same manner as the uneducated Englishman is rendered speechless in the presence of a "gentlemen"; so that an American whose speech is terse, incisive, and functionally adequate when he addresses his own compatriots, becomes pompous, discursive, and inept when conversing with an Englishman of some social prestige. English professors slipping off to America to find relaxation among a supposedly philistine and preeminently colloquial people, find themselves being graciously welcomed to the houses of this and that academician, there to be bored with the most pompous and polysyllabic disquisition upon some "elevated subject." The American professor would never dream of entertaining a confrere in like manner. He would without doubt chat facilely about football and movies, interspersing his conversation with characteristic wisecracks and "Did you hear that one about . . . ?"

Having heard of the dismal experiences of English visitors in this respect and having had one's own in others—winsome girls suddenly changing at the sound of an English accent into reverent devotees of Culture and the Quiet Voice—the Englishman must come to the conclusion that, as far as his speech is concerned, he overawes Americans; and this conclusion is rapidly confirmed by the voluntary admission on the part of most Americans that their brand of English is inferior to the "lovely" English accent.

Philologically, linguistically, historically, nothing of the kind! To repeat: there is no prototype of English, either theoretical or actual; there are only as many individual variations as there are individuals, large numbers of whom fall into roughly homogeneous groups speaking dialects, certain of which by reason of prestige and location happen to be claimed as the "best" English. But such a definition of "best" is wholly arbitrary; whereas in contrast to this arbitrariness stand several inalienable factors: first, that speech is no more and no less than a means of communication; secondly, that dialects all have a common origin and equal historical significance; thirdly, that the only valid criterion for accent is the functional one of intelligibility; and, fourthly, that words are not intrinsically "good" or "bad," but only necessary or redundant.

All that need be added by way of comment is the observation that all these criteria have a fairly objective basis—resting upon the functional adequacy and intelligibility of speech. Hence, if a word like "lousy" or "screwy" or "bughouse" comes up for judgment, it should be reviewed not on the basis of any moral or traditional reactions the adjudicator may experience, but according to its appropriateness and comprehensibility, together with something which might be called linguistic virility. Objectively, then, words such as "lounge lizard," "rubbernecking," "skyscraper," and the like should be adjudged "good" words, recognized as such in the schools, and, where appropriate, used without compunction in private conversation. For teachers of grammar to deplore the use of "lousy," "swell," "cute," and the rest is as ineffectual as the nineteenth century English grammarians' opposition to Americanisms such as "lengthy," "reliable," and "belittle." For people, not academicians, make language.

All this should suggest that the American form of English is as legitimate and valid as English English, but it does not explain the extraordinary prestige of the latter. This phenomenon can be partially interpreted in terms of two characteristic English attributes: thoroughness and lack of imagination. The educated Englishman knows his language so thoroughly that he effectively suppresses any tendencies toward that linguistic inventiveness which distinguishes American speech and writing. Compare, for instance, the English and American use of adjectives. The Englishman will quite naturally prefer seasoned and accepted words where the American will invent a whole new figure of speech. Thus English "perplexed" becomes American "balled up"; English "elegant," American "dolled-up"; a game which is certain of victory in England is "put on ice" in America; and a professor who is invited to edit a dictionary of the American language is, according to American newspaper headlines at least, a "limey prof. imported to dope Yank talk."

The contrast between the two nations' linguistic attitudes is very apparent in their respective journalism, for whereas a constant hullabaloo is the apparent object of the American press, the English strives after dignity and often attains pompousness. To begin with, the more solid English newspapers endorse the attitude of their more solid readers by suppressing any suggestion that there is any news. Those touchy "gents" in clubs who are the chief readers of the more ponderous daily sheets would experience a dangerous rise in their blood pressure if they were shouted at in headlines. They expect to begin the day with a few discreet notices of spas, hot springs, and Mediterranean cruises; then to turn the page and read the official announcements, happenings in the counties, and forthcoming society events; then reports of concerts and theaters; then editorials in parliamentary rhetoric taking the government to task for neglecting rearmament. All this must be interspersed with unsensational news. If an English "gent" should open the *Morning Post* to read a headline with which the *Chicago Tribune* ("world's greatest newspaper") announced a court function as a ceremony at which "Daughters of Democracy Bump Knees for King," he would undoubtedly break a blood vessel and die of apoplexy. And the simultaneous disappearance of hundreds of English gents from the London clubs would probably result in the immediate collapse of the British system.

British journalism, then, of the more dignified school rejects the sensationalism of words and deed which colors the American yellow press with such a yellow yellowness. The London *Times* never shrieks or clamors. Occasionally it thunders in truly Jovian fashion. In the Victorian period it was known as "the Thunderer." Its ominous rumblings and subsequent lightning bolts were feared in every chancery in Europe. But these awe-inspiring detonations were not disguised or interpreted as news. It was the editorial voice. As far as the news was concerned, the *Times* adopted, and still clings to, the quaint British attitude that new news is sufficient (and sufficiently disquieting, for that matter) in itself.

It still bases its reporting on the theory that its readers have some regard for the truth, some sense of proportion, and certain standards of good taste.

But in the early part of the nineteenth century the disquieting influence of America began to be felt upon the English language and journalism. For a time the neologisms which drifted across the Atlantic were roared or thundered or sneered or laughed at according to the temperament of the individual who had newly heard them. In any case, all agreed that an Americanism was a barbarism. There was no doubt about that. Words such as *businessman* and *scientist* caused as much national indignation in their time as the new currency of American slang causes today. It will be remembered what Dean Alford and others thought of American linguistic influences. The contemporary attitude has not changed overmuch. British indignation is still morally righteous in the face of importations such as "You're telling me?" or "You said a mouthful."

Charles Lamb in his day remarked upon the quaintness of American speech, particularly a phrase used by an otherwise charming American girl, namely, "pretty awful." It is ironical to note that "pretty awful" is nowadays a typical expression for derogation in England and has practically disappeared from America. No doubt in fifty years the English will be saying with a bland certainty of correctness, both philological and ethical, "Boy, oh boy, oh boy, if that ain't plain lousy"; to which the answer may well be, "Boy, and how!"

2

Obvious things may be expected, on a little analysis, to be more obscure than obvious. The influence of

American speech on the English language is one of them. It is not at all obvious. There may be a lot; or there may be none. If your philology is based on a nationalistic appraisal of language, you can easily demonstrate that American is now the dominant form of English. You can even talk of an independent American language, as H. L. Mencken does, and go on to prove by references to particular trends the ultimate absorption by American of English English. Or you can ignore national boundaries and regional variations, and speak of a common tongue which is no more "English" or "American" than it is West Saxon or Anglo-Norman.

In this case one recognizes only functional growth, which is not the prerogative of any one group to control. New needs, like new objects, require new words and new expressions. The fact that these neologisms, slang expressions, cant phrases, Americanisms—call them what you will—originate in such and such a place makes no difference whatsoever to their ultimate inclusion in the common stock. The recommendation or disapproval of the grammarians and purists makes even less difference. Carlyle, for instance, coined, used, and presumably advocated certain literal German translations, such as "mischief-joy," by analogy with "Schadenfreude"; Thackeray invented "viduous" from the Latin "viduus" without successfully introducing that word into the language. Yet the obscure and no doubt semieducated Americans who coined the expressions, "bluff," "backwoods," "boardinghouse," "boss," "bunkum," "lounge lizard," "small potatoes," "to bark up the wrong tree," and the rest did make a positive and, nowadays, invaluable addition to the range of thought and expression.

To the extent that the Americans have coined innumerable words and phrases, they have undoubtedly contributed to the English vocabulary. The American linguistic characteristic, indeed, is inventiveness, once the trait of Englishmen. But it would be rash to assume that these contributions have had any basic effect on English—particularly on the written language. Even in the matter of British speech, which is peppered, as it were, with somewhat antiquated American vulgarisms, the effect will probably be short-lived, comparable, perhaps, to the sprinkling of parliamentary oratory in the eighteenth century with Greek quotations and in the nineteenth with Latin tags.

In journalism, however, there is an effect, as much psychological as linguistic. American journalese is a growth independent of the main trunk of the English language. When a sheet such as *Variety* writes, "Pix in Nitery, plus Floor Show at 49 c Convert," we have an entirely new lingo, just as incomprehensible to the American man-in-the-street as to the English professor. But this, after all, is the cant of the stage and falls together with thieves' cant, lumberjacks' language, sailors' talk, printers' signs, and scientific terminology into the class of specialized or guild language. Indeed, *pix* for "pictures" corresponds to *viz.* for "videlicet," both being tironian conveniences no more significant to language than the Pitman or the Gregg system of shorthand. In a few cases the linguistic resourcefulness of a journalist is such that he invents—with far more success than the Carlyles or Thackerays—a personal vocabulary, a daily language in which the majority of words and expressions float down with the other journalistic flotsam to be lost in the sea of yesterday's sensations. Thus, Walter Winchell in inventing the expressions, "the song has oomph!" or "Miss Rita de Leporte, danseuse of the Metopera, will be riveted to Douglas J. Murphy, St. Louis insurance mogul," may be contributing to the gaiety of nations, but it is unlikely that he is influencing the English language. Though brilliant examples of "multum in parvo" such as "the song has oomph!" like Horace's "splendide mendax," may delight students of literature, they can hardly be expected to remain as additions to our language.

Probably American films, far more than American journalism, are exerting their continuous influence on English speech. And what a study in national prejudice is their impact upon an English audience! They sit aghast and uncomprehending, these English, at the quick-fire back chat which American telephone operators apparently exchange in their off moments. They howl with laughter when a tender emotion is couched in a middle-western accent, "Aw, honey, can't yew see I *want* yew." They listen with horror to the harsh threats of gangsters, and finally leave the theater with a hearty disdain of America in general and American speech in particular.

Yet a quiet and, as the English would contend, an alien process goes on all the time in their language. When they use an Americanism in what they think is mockery, it is often in emphasis. The smart set adopt it because it is smart; the lower classes, because of a deficient vocabulary. Slowly the word or the phrase establishes itself. "So and so" is now described as "pretty awful." Then such and such becomes "okay with us." This is pronounced the "tops" instead of "jolly good." That is considered a "pain in the neck" instead of an "awful nuisance." It only remains for the purists to withdraw their moral objections, for the lexicographers to include the word in their dictionaries, and the Americanism will be pronounced indubitably English—and, therefore, irreproachable.

3

Mention was made elsewhere of the parallelism between class and accent in England, and the necessity of the observer's recognizing the latter in order fully to understand the former.

The main class-accent variations can be summed up as follows: Super-Oxonian, or the accent of the public schools; Moderate Oxonian, the accent of the older universities; Standard English, occasionally heard from well-educated people who are not concerned with impressing their listeners; Pseudo-Oxonian, the variation of the suburban or middle-class English; Synthetic Oxonian, or the gallant attempt of "nobodies" to impress their social worth on "somebodies"; uncompromising Cockney, the prevailing accent of the English lower classes; and the dialects, which are becoming increasingly rare. A rough-and-ready guide to these accents is the precision of enunciation the user of them observes in speaking.

There is not much difference in this respect between Super- and Moderate Oxonian, except for the greater loudness and range of the former. Both accents are heard in the clear, high-pitched voices of the upper and upper middle classes. They are impeccable accents, never faltering in their precise enunciation of words. They stand up, moreover, to sudden physical and emotional stress, which will so quickly betray the origins of Pseudo- or Synthetic Oxonian. Genuine Oxonian simply cannot make accentual concessions. It keeps on with its impeccable bleating, whatever the company or whatever the circumstances. "But my deah chap, dewnt you ralize. . . . " It can be imitated quite well by placing a small round stone beneath the tongue, thrusting in the chin, and enunciating the words with a painful meticulousness; and this procedure is recommended to those foreigners who wish to be acceptable in upper and upper-middle-class English circles. For without this emasculated accent one's social worth is highly questionable.

It will be of interest to those foreigners who have been alarmed or annoyed by certain loud English voices, together with glimpses of the speaker's tonsils which seem to accompany them, to know that they were probably listening to genuine Super-Oxonian. For this accent is the only English voice which is so sure of itself as to ignore the traditional national reticence. Indeed, Super-Oxonian is positively brazen in this respect. It will shriek up and down the tonal scale instead of observing the monotone required by English "good form." It has the effrontery to let itself be heard, to make itself public.

The visitor to England can amuse himself by watching the reaction of the other English to a Super-Oxonian voice, raised, for instance, in the solemn confinement of a bus or breaking the chilly silence of a railway carriage. The visitor will see how normal English people shrink into themselves or turn onto the voice the frigid stare of their disapproval. But Super-Oxonian is never abashed. Being the prerogative of extroverts, it feeds on attention, redoubles its volume, reaches a new high on the chromatic scale, and continues to give point to Bright Conversation by such spectacular cries as, "It's absolutely increeedible! Parfectly impooosible!" Super-Oxonian—and this applies to a somewhat lesser extent to the other collegiate varieties—is particularly useful for making those who don't use it feel socially inferior.

Moderate Oxonian is an accent which cannot altogether be helped by the possessors of it. It is characteristic of Oxford (and to some extent of Cambridge) University, which the Super species is not. Moderate Oxonian is, as it were, a little unsure, possibly a little ashamed, of itself. It realizes that it is an aberration from Standard English, an aberration in the direction of affectation and Super-Oxonian, which it does not like at all. Those scholars who stay on at Oxford as tutors soon abandon any pretensions to their undergraduate accent, which so impressed society on the fringes of London. They adopt an easygoing Standard English, which simplifies life considerably. The younger men, fresh from the University, discover that Moderate Oxonian carries considerable weight in the business of getting a job. When, in some desperation, they apply for a housemaster's position in a small private school, the headmaster will immediately inspect their tie, listen carefully to their accent, and say, "Balliol?" or "Christ's?" to which, if they expect to retain his respect, they must be able to answer, "Yes, sir. Perhaps you, too, . . . ?" Moderate Oxonian is very necessary on these occasions. Standard English would not do at all.

Standard English—meaning an accent devoid of affectations and psychological complexes—is exceedingly rare in the British Isles and is quite unknown in the colonies. In those far-flung outposts of the Empire administered by public school men of upper-middle-class extraction, only Super-Oxonian will be heard and reproduced among the natives. Hence, it is not uncommon for a Gold Coast African to speak the most pukkah English, so exquisite, indeed, that a Cockney on hearing it would be automatically petrified into silence, as though in the presence of a gentleman. Moreover, in the "best" places—in the public schools, the foreign consulates, the British clubs abroad, and so on—Standard English would be heartily despised; for the user of it fails to assert his superior status, breeding, education, and occupation. He might be anybody. The puzzled listener is subconsciously irritated by such social nonconformity; for he hears a precise enunciation, a clear delivery, correct grammar, but none of the fireworks upon which his own and other socially superior people's speech relies for its brilliance. Hence, Standard English is seldom accepted as such and seldom appreciated; for, by the same token that it is "good," it will be free from those affectations which arrest the ear of the listener, either dazzling him into thinking he is hearing a beautiful English or annoying him by making his own sound less spectacular. His judgment will depend on his understanding and appreciation of language.

On the subject of Pseudo-Oxonian one can be definite to the extent of relegating it to the middle middle class, the social group which has the direst need of asserting its status. Very few of the middle middle class have been either to a public school or to an older university. Neither Super- nor Moderate Oxonian is native to them. Nor do they have any time for plain, unvarnished Standard English, which will advance them not a whit with Mrs. Anstruthers Carruthers next door, who has just bought a new car apparently with the express purpose of spiting them. But even if they haven't been to Oxford, they can at least give the appearance of having done so; and appearances in suburbia are enough. Unfortunately, however, genuine Oxonian is difficult to mimic well and consistently, particularly if one's natural dialect has certain Cockney elements. The confounded Cockney vowels and initial h's give no end of trouble. And then there is the grammar, which is a very pest. The result of the struggle with sounds and verbs is a garbled version of Super-Oxonian, interspersed with occasional grammatical blunders, the slang current among Society of the last decade, much mouthing of words, flashes of unconscious Cockney, and many bad moments for the speaker. In fact, one may say that the suburban pretender to Oxonian is mentally on tenterhooks every time he opens his mouth. This explains the primness of most of them, the niceness of their English, and the need of their continuous smile.

This Pseudo-Oxonian should be pretty easy for an American to detect, since it is the basis for that peculiar English current on the American vaudeville stage. "Rightho, old choppie! Hang on for a jiffy, will you, old top?" and so forth. Many of these phrases are, as a matter of fact, used by the English suburban middle class, but by no other group in society. If the listener hears this Pseudo-Oxonian, then, he may be reasonably sure that the speaker went to a secondary school, but not to a university; lives in a new house on an unmade street in an unfinished suburb; votes conservative because he is so near the working class; and generally helps stiffen the backbone of England.

To the trained ear there is no mistaking the lowly origin of Synthetic Oxonian, or Careful Cockney, as it might be called; and even the untrained will surely note the speaker's difficulties with aspirates, his uncertain vowels, and the mouthing which he undergoes in order to avoid what he considers the deficiencies of his own dialect. This accent can very nicely be heard from the lips of butlers or Trade Union leaders. It is definitely an education-conscious accent, and the monopoly of the lower classes. It is education-conscious insofar as the user identifies all the material advantages of education, breeding, training, and the rest, which he has been denied, with the accent of gentlemen.

Hence, we find Labor aldermen making huge efforts to sound "refeened," wrestling with vowels, breathing heavily over aspirates, and substituting long words whose meaning they are not altogether certain of for short ones they have used all their lives. So Canning in the panegyric of the borough councillor did not die poor. "'e hexspired in indigunt circumstances." The "educated" chairman does not say a few words; he "begs leave to tender some brief observations." And, according to his report, it was not simply a great crowd which came to see the fire; but "a vast concourse was assembled to witness the 'orrible conflagration." Synthetic Oxonian, or Careful Cockney, can be a great source of satisfaction to the interested observer. A meeting of a London borough council can be recommended. The mayor in his "chines of orfice" is a comfortable figure, typical of a large humanity not found among the sartorially elegant and the linguistically impeccable.

Cockney, of course, is the most self-evident and the most lovable of English accents. Without Cockney all observers would have to admit the complete unhumanity of the English. Without Cockney the wealth and warmth of English literature would be drained away, and little would remain but the somber masterpieces of learned hypochondriacs. Cockney is the most comfortable mode of English expression, used by that section of the people who themselves meet normal standards of comfortable humanity—the English working classes. It has been pointed out, and the fact should be emphasized again, that the English workers are not simply "a strange and interesting portion of the population," as an Italian witness before a parliamentary commission in the middle of the nineteenth century termed them; nor yet a proletarian monster, as foreign observers, such as Taine, considered them. They are as much part of England, as representative of the Islands, as the sartorial caricatures which customarily represent the English abroad. Indeed, it might well be argued that the workers, particularly the rural population, are the last survivors of "Merrie England," retaining that vigorous lust for living, that large appreciation of sensuous things, that quasi-Rabelaisian humor which characterized a noncommercial England of poets, statesmen, and soldiers. The countrymen do not speak Cockney unless the results of elementary education have effectively displaced their dialects by an inferior variety of Standard English which tends to resemble the London speech.

Genuine Cockney can be easily recognized by its peculiar vowel sounds, its laxity with medial consonants, and its special vocabulary. For Standard English "butter," the Cockney would prefer "bu'er," with which may be compared the American variant "buder." And sufficient to observe that "bu'er," "buder," and "butter" are all equally legitimate developments from the same origin, whatever that may have been.

It is in their vocabulary and expressions that the Cockneys evince that warmness and humanity which some critics deny to the whole English people on the grounds of the peculiarities of one section of them. The Cockney considers no one an enemy. To him strangers, foreigners, and aliens alike are "mytes" (mates) and sometimes "cocks." A Cockney will sit in a French café, look around with unrepressed pleasure at his surroundings, direct at an astonished Frenchman a very large wink, and observe to the obsequious waiter, "Fine dy, myte! Crikey! Mykes yer glad ter be alive. Bring me an yle, that's a peach." Nothing frigid or formal about this, either in the mode of address or the feeling behind it. The Cockney is everybody's friend.

One feature of Cockney lingo will serve to illustrate the good humor and amiability of both their speech and their psychology. It is their riming slang. A list of these peculiar circumlocutions, carefully collected in many a barroom and workshop, is appended herewith for the wonder and admiration of all students of language and human nature alike.

Cockney and dialects, factory workers and farm laborers, must be taken into account in any true estimate of the soul of England. For they constitute the little island's chief claim to humanity. Millions of humble people, unobserved, apparently, by foreign tourist and student, pursue their amiable way, retaining in a damp and frigid land those most precious of human traits, generosity and sociability.

Standard English	Cockney	Standard English	Cockney
boots	daisy roots	fire	Anna Maria
cheese	stand-at-ease	stairs	apples and pears
hat	tit-for-tat	sick	Uncle Dick
neck	bushel and peck	floor	Rory o' Moore
feet	plates o' meat	beer	pig's ear
park	coppers nark	socks	Tilbury Docks
wife	drum and fife	eyes	kidney pies
kid	God forbid	hair	Barnet fair
walk	ball o' chalk	pipe	cherry ripe
sun	currant bun	balls	orchestra stalls
road	frog and toad	coat	line and float
money	bees and honey	old man	old pot and pan
gin	needle and pin	bread	strike me dead
nose	I suppose	butter	roll in the gutter

Let the critic take them into account in his judgment of the English—if for no other reason than for such contributions to language as *plates of meat* for *feet; bees and honey* for *money; kidney pies* for *eyes;* and, sublime humanity! *drum and fife* for *wife.*

138

XI

Journalism

I

THE trouble with English journalism is English literature. Ever since their language reached its maturity and, as far as they were concerned, ceased to develop, the English have adopted toward it a reverential attitude which contrasts sharply with the way they thumped and tortured and contorted it in larger days. The pre-Elizabethans conducted all manner of experiments upon it: they alternately Anglicized, Latinized, and Frenchified it. The university wits assaulted it with their ungovernable passion. The churchmen hurled the dictionary at each other's heads with all the fervor of the imperious ecclesiast. In the seventeenth and eighteenth centuries the rhetoricians blew it up with their windy Latinisms, whose monstrous pomposities the essayists proceeded to prick with rapier witticisms.

All these experiments, transitions, changes are regarded now as the history of the English language and literature, whose last chapter was written by Messrs.

Carlyle, Ruskin, and Walter Pater. The clumsiest or wildest or most grotesque developments of our ancestors are regarded with all the awe the English yield to antiquity. Marlowe's bombast is condoned on the strength of a couple of "mighty lines"; Shakespeare's rant and jingles are explained away by critically emasculated commentators. Thomas Browne is excused his funereal Latinisms, Dr. Johnson his "polysyllabic propensities" —all because these mortals have been apotheosized by unimaginative textbook writers; or, more simply, because they lived before 1800, at which date all decent historians of the English language and literature terminate their studies. But the comparable experiments, adaptations, abuses, and the rest which are alleged in the English language today, and particularly the American branch of it, are not tolerated for a moment—on the grounds, ironically enough, that they are not in keeping with the heritage of the language. This attitude toward language is rather like that of the conservative American's attitude toward revolution—inconsistent to say the least.

So we find that English journalism today is preeminently dignified, strenuously respectable, and unmistakably stodgy. Although it is presumably dealing with a new age, new events, and new attitudes of mind, its reports are worded in the language of the nineteenth century on the tacit assumption that English style reached its apex in the parliamentary oratory which reverberated through the houses of Parliament toward the end of that period. It contrasts painfully with the contemporary journalism of America—painfully, at least, for those who adopt the reverential attitude toward language on the basis that it is an artifact to be preserved intact like a relic in a museum.

Unfortunately for the effect and the efficacy of British journalism the standard laid down has been based on one of the most pompous and ineffectual periods in English life and letters; and the two, as we might expect, are inextricably bound together. Where the mentality of an age is naïve, the language will be naïve; where sanctimonious, the language will be sanctimonious; where adventurous, the language adventurous. But the late nineteenth century was, on the whole, a pretty sterile or, possibly, constipated period. It lacked the naïveté or fearlessness or passion which distinguished earlier periods of the national history, and substituted a smug, stuffy point of view which best expressed itself in cant.

Speaking in Parliament of the awful poverty and hardships which were then prevalent in England, Mr. Cobden declared: "The Angel of Death is abroad tonight. You can almost hear the beating of his wings." This was considered, and rightly, very fine rhetoric, but it was not what a person who felt passionately and indignantly would say. Rather, these were the words of a gentleman, warm, comfortable, and self-assured—intent on impressing his hearers with a pretty figure of speech. And today, when a leading British paper reports the abdication of a once beloved monarch in these words: "This great cynosure institution, round which as their sole remaining formal centre the shining constellation of the British Commonwealth revolves, cannot itself be grounded on a peradventure," we must assume that the writer is more concerned with maintaining the journalistic reputation of the *Sunday Times* than expressing his feelings—whose existence we may legitimately suspect.

We might note this possibility. It is possible that British newspapers and the other ephemeral publications are concerned not only with expressing themselves in a dignified manner, but also with avoiding the statement of any strong feeling. They do, possibly, report quite adequately the half-emotions which they feel. And we should not forget that they are the voice of the British public.

One begins to realize this fact in the face of direct evidence such as this. In writing of women, the *Sunday Times* is speaking for the British public, as well as raising its own dignified voice, when it says: "Unlike so many women who see in themselves nothing more than a logical, biological necessity, Princess von Bismarck is charmingly excited at being a woman." "Charmingly excited" is significant; not emotionally stirred, mind you, not passionately aware of the fact, not smarting under the implications, uncompromisingly rebellious, or merely indifferent—but "*charmingly excited.*" What can this mean other than that she fits into the average Englishman's conception of the place of women in society: that she flutters in his presence, that she accepts first his gratuitous flattery, and then his expensive terms? Thus does British journalism reveal, with a kind of dignified coyness, both its own and its public's mind. It is fundamentally nineteenth century.

We might plunge, then, at a generalization, and say that British journalism reflects fairly clearly prevailing British attitudes. Sex, patriotism, jingoism, British superiority, religious convictions are all displayed for the foreign observer who takes the trouble to examine the newspapers. If he wants to understand the relation of sport to the national character, he might ponder over this bit of journalistic evidence:

"They saved General Franco," reads a caption under the photograph of one Major Hugh Pollard, his daughter, and a lady identified as Ann Other. "It takes good foxhunters to do a job like this."

If he wants a glimpse of religion, Calvinistic and Church of England, he should weigh the implications of these reports:

At a meeting on Monday night of the Aberystwyth Free Church Council Mr. David Phillips said that the B.B.C. had been broadcasting gardening talks on Sunday. They in Wales regarded that as a sacrilege and something which jarred on the ears of Welshmen. It was not in any way elevating to hear that sort of thing on a Sunday. . . .

and Church of England: (this is the Bishop of Portsmouth reported in the *Isle of Wight Chronicle*):

In England they learned long ago that they must work as a team and sink their personal interests for the good of the community. The first public school man had been born in Nazareth, and his name was Jesus Christ; the second was his disciple, St. Paul.

The choice of the two candidates here accepted in the ranks of public school men is noteworthy. Jesus Christ, like his Father, is able to crash British society on the strength of his alleged aristocratic descent; and blood will tell. St. Paul had the double advantage of being well-born and a member of the Church. He is the kind of person who would look well in gaiters. In the case of those who were a bit too Hebraic, such as Moses; too irregular, such as King Solomon; or too low-bred, such as the other disciples, neither British society nor its public schools could tolerate them for a moment. The Pharisees, not being as other men, would be acceptable. They would fit excellently into the best English society. Those men of God who rose no higher in the ranks than lake fishermen would have to be promoted to something in the navy; and if they could then learn how to cover up their proletarian accent with a gun-turret roar, they would be presentable in the more crusty groups of high life.

English patriotism, journalistic version, is of two kinds: the bulldog breed and the "we don't want to fight, but by jingo if we do" variety—the aggressive and the modest species. The foreign critic will acquire a considerable understanding of the British character by searching the newspapers for examples of national bombast. Not that he will have to search far, if he goes to the right sources. If he wants the barking of the bull-dog breed, he should listen to the clamor of *The Saturday Review*, to such sentiments as this, for example, yelped by Lady Houston on the occasion of the abdication of King Edward VIII:

We want *you*, sire; *you*, our King. The others are enemies, false and treacherous as hell—who are working to drag you and your people down to destruction by bringing war on the nation they have unarmed.

Wise men do not despise the counsel of a woman; hear me then, oh! my king, for I love you and every word I write is the inspired truth; that is why they fear me.

I have put my whole heart and soul into telling the people of England facts that these leaders hide from them. For I belong to the bulldog breed and I not only bark but bite the enemies within our midst.

It is a strange country, this England. Some women delighting in being "charmingly exciting"; others considering unchastity the most terrible thing that could happen to them; others barking and biting.

The barkings of a Lady Houston, however, are much too loud and brazen to be characteristic of Britain's voice today. After all, the still louder snarls of younger and more energetic nationalists, who not only conduct themselves like dogs, but particular rabid dogs at that, call for a counsel of the occasional growl. The English have substituted the still, small voice of righteousness for the old bulldog roar. "Stay away from our kennel"; they say, "Leave us our bone; and go and worry some other dog."

Our Air council, we are told, has decided never to bomb open towns—unless overruled on the matter by a War Cabinet. Our experts believe that such massacres simply serve to stiffen the resistance of the enemy. Our bombing will be of railways, etc. . . .

There are exceptions, of course, to every rule. The open villages of the Indian hillsmen are one exception. But, on the whole, patriotic utterances of this kind are compromising rather than belligerent—the grunt of an old dog rather than the yelp of a young one.

2

The American influence in all departments of British life is no more evident than in British journalism. Although we hear American ways and American words continually disparaged by the more English of the English, although editors of newspapers frown upon Americanisms as crude, the techniques and psychology of American journalistic practice have largely determined the more modern of British newspapers today. Such papers, the penny dailies, make considerable efforts to be as alive and as lively as the events they are reporting. They even make efforts to be tabloidish, with the result that their manner is often skittish, their style a cross between nineteenth century English rhetoric and twentieth century American wisecracks.

They are on surer ground when it comes to the subject matter of tabloid journalism, for they have learned the lesson so ably demonstrated by William Randolph Hearst: that crime and underwear are the major topics of human interest. They are fortunate, too, in this respect. Both phenomena are less numerous and less commonplace in English than in American life. American newspapers are obliged to dismiss ten or more homicides as so many fillers among more spectacular happenings; and dainty lingerie is no more mysterious to American men than the women who get into it. In America crime must be accompanied by some particularly exotic circumstances: there must be a half-filled bath with cigarette butts at each end; or evidence of a struggle in order to introduce the rape *motif;* or a very rich man and a hard-up chorus girl in order that the fornication might be obvious. And underclothes must be filled out with swelling curves that leave no uncertainty as to what they promise, if only one had the money to buy the necessary silver fox fur.

In America, where crime is organized on a grand scale and professional criminals behave as though they were enacting a film for the benefit of the American public, where a large proportion of females conduct themselves as though they were born with the sole function of being photographed in bathing costume—in America both crime and underwear have to be presented in the press without any attempt to spoil the fun with moral censure. American journalism leaves nothing to be desired in its painstaking and unprejudiced reporting of what is meretricious beneath the surface of society, and beneath the covering of an evening gown.

In England, however, these revelations are pretty terrific things—both being alike unseemly, as it were. However, it is too much to ask of even an English newspaper to resist reporting the details of a crime in which a body is found in four sections in four different places; or a dancer has her legs insured for five hundred thousand pounds. The parts of the body must be enumerated, the legs photographed. Nonetheless, the English newspaper cannot throw morality and caution to the winds in the manner of the American tabloid. It must protect itself from public indignation by assuming (or possibly even feeling) such indignation itself. The quadrated body becomes in the British press a Brutal Murder, a Horrible Crime, and is written up as though the editors were reporting the decapitation of their own aunts. In this way the Gruesome Details can be carried on the front page from day to day, not as vicarious thrills, but in the cause of public safety. The trial and emotions of the defendant can be transcribed fully in the cause of justice; as much of the hanging scene as possible, as an example of retribution. The newspaper takes good care to vindicate its own and the reader's virtue. Theirs is no vulgar curiosity, but a feeling of proper revulsion, of social solidarity, of justice, of righteousness.

For sex—possibly *sexiness* would be a better word— the same method of self-justification is employed. The dancer's legs, as though indecent in themselves (according to British morality, the thoughts connected with them are)—the dancer's legs are merely incidental to the supposedly interesting fact that they are insured for five hundred thousand pounds. Where something more than a view of knees and calves is desired, the English rely on the "health-and-beauty" magazines, which flourish in untold numbers on the bookstands. The subterfuge of the "body beautiful" (and semidenuded) has been picked up from shrewd American publications. The French could offer a solution in the overtly salacious type of magazine; but the English would not tolerate palpable nudity (with a joke appended) for a moment. "Health-and-beauty" was the solution. Further, in keeping with the dignity of English life, the facts usually confined to police gazettes in the United States are incorporated into "sex-problem" magazines in England. Each week these shrewd publications catch the hopeful introvert with a headline implying some explanation of the sexual function, decently written up by "M.D." and scrupulously avoiding any positive (and hence indecent) information.

This inordinate scatological curiosity of the English about sex is not simply a matter of journalistic muck-raking. It is something more fundamental and signifi-cant. It does, however, determine certain aspects of British journalism. It explains certain characteristic developments. If we compare the popular American Sunday newspapers with the English, for instance, we can see that while the Americans are presumably in-terested in reading on topics ranging from popular ac-counts of astronomy to the pointless adventures of some obnoxious youth in a comic strip, the English are pro-vided only with accounts of divorces and criminal as-saults to read over their morning eggs and bacon. A Sunday paper such as *The News of the World* is, in spite of its comprehensive title, simply a news of petty venery: page after page of it, all eagerly devoured by thousands of sex-curious Britons lying in bed on Sunday mornings.

It might rightly be claimed that, compared to Ameri-can journalistic extravagances, English newspapers are positively mild and innocuous. This may be true. It is certainly true that the front page of an English daily does not look, in the manner of a Hearst publication, like the case histories of a number of asocial maniacs. It is also true that crime is presented not as the regu-lar and "to-be-continued" entertainment of a million readers, as it is in a country which idealizes its more vicious criminals. It is true again that legs, bosoms, rumps, feminine mysteries, masculine weaknesses, and the rest of the subventral activities are treated with a certain delicacy in the English press, whereas they are barked up in American journalism with all the lack of finesse associated with a small-town sideshow. These things are true; but not so certain is the ultimate perniciousness of the two national methods. This is not a matter for an observer, but for a philosopher to decide; and in his case it might depend on a choice between muckraking with a steam shovel and muckraking with a colander.

To understand the English, it is well to look at them in the mirror of their own journalism, with some of these observations in mind.

XII

Humor

IT IS possible that the English have no sense of
humor—outside their own longitudes. It is certain
that they have no sense of humor according to American standards. In fact, what passes for humor among
the English is often positively annoying to Americans,
and to other peoples for that matter. But since humor,
or at least the formal expression of it, is largely a matter
of language, the other nationalities are not bothered
overmuch with or about English humor. The French,
the Italians, the Chinese, the West Africans, all suppose that the English brand of humor is like the English brand of suet pudding, something too alien or too
gross for them to stomach.

The Americans, however, are bothered—profoundly,
worryingly, even unhappily bothered. First of all, there
is the Englishman's confounded verbal ingenuity—his
wit, his darting, facile terminology, his cynical, icono-
clastic *facetiae*—which to the American is, if not exactly
distressing, at least bewildering. What, for instance, is
he to reply to an individual who takes the words out
of his mouth before he has had time to announce them

himself; or takes his words, sets them up as targets, and riddles them with the fire of some verbal cannonade? "As far as I know," says the American, "we're perfect strangers." "Quite," shoots back the Englishman, "except that none of us is perfect." (His grammar is, though, confound him.) "Are you married, then?" asks the American. "No," replies the Englishman, "I've made every proposal to a woman so far except matrimony." Verbal ingenuities. Conjuring tricks with words. But not humor.

The fact is, the Englishman will be facetious or irreverent at the expense of the things the American regards with sentiment or with awe. And this is not funny to the latter. For there are certain objects and concepts, such as culture and motherhood, which the representative American approaches as he approaches his Constitution. He pulls a long face and puts himself in a rhetorical frame of mind. He will go to a lecture, for instance, expecting to be uplifted or harangued or simply bored, but certainly not to be amused. The Englishman goes in the opposite frame of mind: censorious and cynical, alert to detect platitudes and inaccuracies, providing aloud or to himself a running commentary of apt, and often carping, criticism.

Hence, that type of English wit which mocks at American sanctities is not considered funny in the United States, although it is highly successful at home. English wits from Charles Dickens to Bernard Shaw have found this to their cost. For, strictly in keeping with the English sense of humor, they have laughed where they were expected to console, dropped a witticism instead of a condolence. Not only do Americans not think this funny; they have adjudged it definitely bad taste.

On the other hand, the Englishman will contribute nothing to that prosaic geniality which typifies the American sense of fun. If there is no occasion for incidental wit, he shuts his mouth tight on both words and laughter. Isolated wisecracks, jokes, horseplay leave him cold and grim when the American is most uproarious. Nor does he have the amiability or the naïveté to laugh when the others laugh, to assume that expression of expectant merriment at the beginning, and to maintain it throughout, a long and involved anecdote with which the American likes to liven his conversation. If the Englishman is given time to explain his absence of merriment on these occasions, he might reply that, even if he has not heard the story in a dentist's copy of a funny paper, he has seen the point ten minutes before the teller arrives at it himself. Once again, if given the chance, he can substitute for a lack of humor a terse, incisive witticism at the expense of somebody else.

If his mental processes could be analyzed during one of these after-dinner jokes, it would be found that his intellectual honesty or his formality had been too shocked to admit of participation in what he regards as a pose. What has this story got to do with God and Science; or with the American Contribution to Architecture; or with How to Be Happy though Married, he is asking himself. And how can all these people sit in rows around a dinner table and laugh together in such an open manner for such a long time? Why should the speaker make a monkey of himself in order to arrest the attention of his listeners? Why, in brief, are Americans so afraid of being bored and of boring that they have to be consciously and conscientiously funny? The social implications, it will be seen, are uppermost in his mind. His strong sense of the fitting precludes his appreciation of the ridiculous—in public.

All this amounts to the probability that the Englishman cannot be humorous at the expense of his dignity. He hates, for instance, to be the "life of the party." He hates, as an individual, to be the center of attraction. Witty conversation of the English genre is purely impersonal. One listens to the words without being aware of the personality of the teller. Faces can thus continue to wear the impenetrable mask in keeping with good form. But to assume the role of a circus clown or the village idiot or even a professional raconteur is as abhorrent to the Englishman as slipping on a banana peel in public or losing his hat on the street. It is too much of a strain on his shyness.

However, as with everything else English, generalizations must be modified to meet the inevitable variations caused by class differences. The verbal ingenuity which is characteristic of the educated Englishman of the upper and upper-middle-class group, should not be expected in the conversation of a middle- or lower class person. The former in his unconscious striving after mediocrity avoids any phrase, as any action, which might single him out as unusual; the latter's vocabulary is too deficient for the play of wit.

Of the three main classes it is apparently the bourgeoisie which has given the English so disastrous a reputation in the matter of humor. And rightly so, judging from the attempts at it which are brought to the attention of foreigners. The national journal of humor, for instance: that incredible publication known as *Punch*. "Green peas have done well this year," titters *Punch*. "There has also been some grand weather for ducks." "There is a circus clown who rides a mule back to front while blindfolded, and juggles with four ping-pong balls. Sir Walter Gregory is, we understand, not in favor of his appearing in Rotten Row." And, "A linguist has impressed us with the fact that there are several ways of pronouncing Bzrlski. Nevertheless, we shall persist in pronouncing it Bzrlski."

One should note the exemplary discretion of these squibs. They are calculated, as it were, to encourage a snigger rather than a guffaw. They are strictly in good taste: discreet and noncommittal, perfectly in keeping with that great middle-class sense of humor, which abjures anything too subtle, anything too piquant, anything too noisy. Hence satire, cynicism, and irony are ill-suited to pages of *Punch*. Not general human weaknesses, but the misfortunes of certain despised types are smiled at. These are the representatives of the classes the comfortable and respectable most resent, because they most socially resemble; notably the more tame of the lower classes.

The socially abnormal are also fair game, on the grounds that they have a way of making material comfort and respectability seem unmitigably dull and stodgy. Add to the despised or discomforting types a little gentle humor at the expense of oneself, and you have the formula of England's most representative humorous journal, *Punch*. Hence, the servant girl, disheveled and distraught in the presence of her so superior mistress: "Oh, if you please, 'm, Cook's very sorry, 'm, but she can't get the soufflé to lather." Hence, the char-woman on her bony knees, with ill-kempt hair and man's cap, singing in the presence of the suburban housewife, "When somebody thinks you're *won-der-ful*." Hence, the plumber, the tramp, the milkman, the oldest inhabitant, and the Cockney flapper. Hence the highbrow . . . *He:* "Have you read much George Bernard Shaw?" *She:* "No, but I think I know who you mean." And hence, a little sly humor at the expense of the peppery colonel, the suburban gardener, and the kiddies. . . . *First child:* "Joan told me a dreadful story and frightened me." *Second child:* "Yes—(blub)—and I've frightened myself, too."

People who read *Punch* and whose standards of hu-mor are based on social gradations have no time for guffaws or belly laughter. Those hearty masterpieces of English humor which were written in palmier days appeal to them not at all. If they had the courage to say so, Shakespeare with his Falstaffs, his Bully Bottoms (the very name distresses them), and his company of pimps, jesters, and winebibbers, is plainly vulgar. For-tunately ignorance keeps Chaucer, Rabelais, and the classical humorists from them. Only among the lower classes, in those music halls which hand on the tradi-tion of ribaldry, are the basic weaknesses and incon-gruities of mankind laughed at with gusty and primitive laughter. But such weaknesses and incongruities smack too much of the more animal and less ennobling char-acteristics of his own nature to suit the individual whose life is ruled by the dictates of godliness and cleanliness. They are altogether too functional and crude.

The members of the great British middle class, that pillar of English society, do not want to be shaken by mirth or cleansed by it. Both procedures they would consider quite superfluous in their particular cases. They want to be amused, but amused at the proper time. In their well-ordered minds humor has its place, carefully shut off from other matters, such as religion and washing and visiting one's neighbors. It can easily become exaggerated out of keeping with a respectable mode of existence. And if it is not the occasion for humor, they are offended by having it thrust upon their attention. There is a time and place for everything, is one of their unwritten laws. The place for humor is in the jokes of professional humorists and in the pages of special journals; the time, when there are no more pressing matters to be considered.

Yet there is running through the whole of that English life which is less pretentious and less circumscribed—among those members of society who are not dehumanized in their efforts to keep up an appearance—an undercurrent of humor which transcends almost every other national characteristic. It is evidenced in the writings of those great humanitarians from the time of Chaucer through Shakespeare, Fielding, Dickens, to the time of James Joyce, in that body of English literature which taps the inexhaustible springs of laughter. It is evidenced more prosaically in the twist of the nose or the lift of the eyebrow of almost every English commoner who has not been drained of his native sprightliness by hunger and idleness.

Laughter bellows forth in every inn and public house. Quips, jokes, jibes, drolleries spring to the lips of those humble people who carry weights on their backs, maneuver carts through the streets, take ships down the rivers, or drive their cattle to country markets. That servant girl or charwoman who amuses the supercilious suburban housewife in the pages of *Punch* is actually living the humor which has made the reputation of Dickens. The plumber's conversation is not confined to asserting his plebeian superiority to the helpless householder in the matter of a leak in the bath pipe. He saves his observations for his mates in "The Bricklayers Arms." The oldest inhabitant leaning on his cottage gate is not there for the express purpose of making some inane remark to the vicar, but is more likely turning a dry jest at the expense of the urbanized and prudish. And the Cockney flapper is not dropping her aitches for the amusement of people who make such an effort to retain them, but is crystallizing her philosophy of life in a pithy quip which would send the novelist running to his scrapbook.

These things should be remembered. The psychological limitations in funny magazines such as *Punch* are only one aspect of British humor. On almost every street corner and village square there are living examples to offset such smugness. Moreover, for those English minds which have transmuted, as it were, humor into wit, self-conscious attempts to incite laughter will be tedious; hence, the ineffectualness of the American story for those Englishmen who have to suffer it at dinner parties. And hence the Englishman's frozen expression. The obvious is never funny, and wit is better never than late. Because humor is an attitude of mind, the suspicion of the comical in the familiar, the Englishman cannot be expected to laugh at a reference to the Empire State Building. To assert that he has no sense of humor because he does not, is to betray an ignorance of English character and geography. The British Isles are not yet a department of New York City; nor is English humor measurable in terms of the comic strip.

Book III

LIFE

XIII

Work and Play

The History of Bill and Ethel Grimes

BILL Grimes is a docker down at the Surrey Commercial Docks, Rotherhithe, London. An occasional Cunarder berths there, a one-funneled, eighteen thousand tonner, Montreal to London; but far more numerous and important from Bill's point of view are the Norwegian timber ships which arrive every other day, some of them with a list of twenty degrees when they have met rough weather in the North Sea.

Bill Grimes, to be specific, is a deal porter. If you examined his right shoulder, you would find a huge callous along the scapula, and this in spite of the special leather padding in his working coat. You would realize why, if you had seen Grimes transporting three twelve-foot planks at once from the hold of a timber ship to the woodyard. With his head bowed slightly forward and to the left, he swings along a narrow wooden plank, timing his steps to the rebound of the perilous gangway.

Grimes earns good money, working from eight in the morning to four in the evening, with handsome com-

163

pensation for overtime. His trade union, the waterside laborers, is a strong one. They can easily tie up the whole activity of London by a strike, since most of the movement and prosperity of London centers in its mighty wharves and the constant coming and going of ships. Sometimes, in the event of a strike, the medical students, in search of fun, undertake the unloading of ships; but half an hour of plank hauling is enough for most of them, especially if a comrade falls from the elastic gangway into the sooty water between ship and dock.

Grimes is a typical English workingman, and looks it. As a matter of fact, he looks tougher than he really is, both figuratively and literally. His clothes are old, ragged, and dirty. A black choker takes the place of collar and tie. A cap is pulled well down over his narrow forehead. His face is shaven, but not particularly well washed. It is white and a bit hollow about the cheekbones. Inadequate food and lack of sunshine are responsible for this, not any constitutional debility. The conditions under which Bill was born and grew up preclude the survival of any but the constitutionally fit. The tenements in Rotherhithe and Greenwich from which he and his kind come forth in the mornings are the solid evidence of those conditions. One might almost presume that they were built with the express purpose of debilitating the working-class stock. To begin with, they are architecturally as hideous as possible: flat, gray, boxlike structures, with dark, narrow stairs which effectively exhaust any tenant over thirty years of age and cause pregnant women to gasp for breath on the fifth of the eight flights. The windows are small and most of them abut onto another building, the architects apparently having a cynical preference for a background of soap or pickle factories.

Bill Grimes lives on the fourth floor of Winsor Buildings. With him live his wife, her mother, two children (another one expected maybe), and one lodger. There are three rooms—kitchen, bedroom, parlor. The family share a toilet with the two other families on the fourth landing, and much ill feeling results—particularly after the week-end "binge" in which the Sheens across the landing indulge. For Mrs. Grimes refuses to clean up after Mr. Sheen—even though it is her turn; and Mrs. Hobbs doesn't do a proper job when it's her week. As Mr. Hobbs, an unemployed communist, so aptly observes, "the 'ole arryngement's another bloody capitalist crime."

Within Bill Grimes's flat, then, live seven people, one of them comparatively snug (being unborn), the rest all pretty much in each other's way. The lodger, of course, has precedence, although Grimes mutteringly resents this, especially when the outsider gets a bit of meat and he gets only tinned salmon. But as the missus says, he may be out of work next week, and then they'll need that twenty-five bob forked out weekly by young Mr. Layman. So "young Mr. Layman" sleeps by himself on the living room couch and gets a bit of meat when the others get tinned salmon. Mrs. Grimes, aged thirty-three, pale and blotchy, pronounces him no trouble, no trouble at all. As he is courting, he is out every night of the week gallivanting around with his girl—a fast cat in Mrs. Grimes's opinion; but then that's none of her business.

Mrs. Grimes's history is typical enough of about ten million other working-class women in England. Those who know it will agree that her life is more work than play, and more drudgery than work. Her fun was over for good and all when she married Bill Grimes. She was nineteen. And with her fun went her youth and comeliness, thanks largely to Winsor Buildings and Mr. Grimes's demands after 11 P.M. Before her marriage Ethel Grimes—or Effie Watson as she was then—worked in a biscuit factory which gave the impression, to visitors at least, of being a model institution, what with its library, theater, fire brigade, and the rest. Ethel Watson was in the packing department and worked on a piece-time schedule; but although her fingers were leaping around from eight to five in order to earn twenty-six shillings a week, the rest of her energy was unabsorbed, so that when she issued forth from the works on the five o'clock whistle, she was all ready for a good time. Ethel's idea of a good time was the same as every working-class girl's in England.

First, a large tea was consumed round six when the rest of the family had gathered about the table. At this ceremony Ethel enjoyed a quarrel with her younger brother, Bert, and a few "words" with her father. Like all the other girls at the biscuit factory, she made it a point to cheek her father in order to demonstrate her independence. And independent she considered herself on the strength of her twenty-six shillings a week, fourteen of which her mother collected, two of which went into a girl's club, leaving ten to buy all the liberty a girl of eighteen could desire. This liberty was embodied in red hats, "Lady Jane's" face powder, and a seat in a West-end cinema.

After tea—consisting of large quantities of bread and butter, fish paste, fly-blown pastries, and several cups of strong tea—Ethel rushed from the table before her father had time to lecture her or her mother to catch her for washing up.

Not troubling to wash her face, she repaired any ravages which London soot had made on her smooth skin by the addition of "Lady Jane" powder, dabs of "kisspruf" rouge, and a crude attempt at mascara. Mr. Watson, who "didn't 'old with no lamp black" (as he called it), thought she was coming it a bit too much. But in the interval that her father was picking his teeth with a fork and meditating on the racing news, Ethel had clamped a beret on her head and shot down the stairs into the romantic gloom of the London streets.

The London streets! They offered her complete freedom and exquisitely improbable adventures. These she sought in company with her friends, Madge Butcher and Lizzie Dean. Madge and Lizzie give the impression of having been cast in identically the same mold as Ethel herself. Their interests, pleasures, and hopes are substantially the same. Each of them wears a beret, uses the same cosmetics with the same lack of artistry, talks on the same subject—boys—and hopes to achieve the same object—marriage, not with a "boy," but with a "gent."

For males in the classification of Ethel, Madge, and Lizzie fall into two and only two classes: "gents" and "boys." Their idea of the former is as uncomplicated and direct as their experience with the latter. A "gent" is a male who raises his hat to you in the street, like the Vicar at St. James's. A "gent" says "How do you do?" when he meets you instead of "Wotcher Effel!" A "gent" says clever things and smiles at you; a "boy" is always after the same thing—even in his conversation, and gets nasty when you push him away. A "gent" takes you in a taxi; a "boy," in a train. A "gent" raises his hat at your front door, says good-night, and goes; a "boy" begins to "muck you about" and keeps you out so that Dad bawls at you for getting in after eleven-thirty. "Gents" never marry you; "boys" always do.

In their hearts, Ethel and Madge and Lizzie know why. Their accent, for instance, is the crudest Cockney, their jokes come from the music hall, their laughter is as raucous as that of the "boys" they despise. But they don't know any "gents," and they all know the same boys and where to find them: on the corner by the pawnbroker's, outside the public library, in the park by the bandstand. Hence, Ethel, Madge, and Lizzie's manner of walking the streets is an invariable ritual. They know which men to ogle, which to glare at, which to stop and joke with. They know exactly the significance of the whistles, clucks, and twitterings of the youths who rove the streets in search of prey such as girls like them.

All this, in spite of the secret hopes and longings connected with "gents," is the substance of romance and adventure to the three girls, culminating on Saturday nights in a dance at the Town Hall or a visit to the "picshers" with a new "boy." It was at a carnival dance that Ethel met Bill Grimes. She met him in the bar when she was a bit "fuzzy." He finished off the process of befuddlement, and then began the assault upon her which ended on what her parents considered the respectable side of the altar.

All this was unalloyed amusement to Ethel. Roaming the streets, dancing, telling off "boys," Saturday night parties, kissing in passages—an eternal round of pleasures. Even the biscuit factory was fun, much more so than the elementary school, at any rate. She was always joking with the other girls and hoping one of the clerks in the office would take her out, which one eventually did, with almost disastrous results.

The first four months of marriage were all right, although Ethel's ignorance of the most elementary sexual matters and Bill's inexperience caused between them a good many rows, necessitating the girl's spending several nights back under her mother's roof. Then Bill was advised by her father "to lay off the girl for a bit; to be decent, and all that, you know," and things were easier for Ethel. She could amuse herself in those early days by entertaining her girl friends and pointing out the furniture, acquired on the deferred payment system. This was all right as long as Bill was in work, of course. When he fell idle, they had to take in the lodger, of whom Grimes was surlily jealous, although his wife was now eight months gone with child, and in his opinion (hoarsely confided to his mates at the *Royal Arms*) as "cold as the side of a ship."

After her first child, the play and fun and youthfulness which had romanticized even the endless and dreary streets of Ethel's London ceased for good. Her friends were no longer interested in her. She never roamed the streets ogling or glaring at the "boys." It wasn't decent. She never went to dances. Bill wasn't interested. He preferred a pint of beer with a lot of rough dockers. Ethel took to dreaming again of "gents." Staring at herself in the scullery mirror, she thought there still might be a chance. In the meanwhile, there were the pleasures of the "picshers" and the saloon bar; the lovely romance of Madge Evans at the *Majestic* and the lethargy induced by a Guinness at the *Royal Arms*.

And thus Bill and Ethel Grimes produced a numerous progeny, all the time growing older and more hopeless, themselves. The husband went onto relief, the wife allowed the dirt to accrue in the dark kitchen. But their children grew apace, full of the vitality and the eagerness which once had activated their parents. The boys followed the youthful pastimes of their father, the girls, those of their mother. They roamed the streets which their parents had roamed, chasing or being chased. They frequented the same dance halls and fell in love under much the same conditions. In due course they married, bought their furniture on the installment system, bore children, and settled down into domestic indifference.

Multiply the process by ten million, and you have the work and play of the English lower classes.

XIV

It Raineth Every Day

THE foreign observer will be able to see as much of this dismal process as he will probably want by a day's visit to one of the less salubrious districts of London, or of any other big manufacturing city. He can take a bus from his West-end hotel and from its upper deck overlook the East end. This is an easy, almost a pleasant method of geographical and social survey; but even if it gives a good idea of the city slums, it cannot give the feel of them. And it is this *feel* which distinguishes an English slum from those of other countries.

To get atmosphere, the visitor must walk, as the dwellers in the gray, barracklike tenements and those in the hovellike cottages walk. For it is the interminable streets which seem to be so characteristic of an English city—the long, gray streets and the complete absence of color. There are slums in Marseille, Paris, Berlin, Chicago, and Buenos Aires which are more dilapidated, stricken, and shameful to a civilized people; but there is nothing comparable to the unmitigated dreariness, to the almost impenetrable gloom which rest upon the depressed industrial centers of Great Britain.

If the visitor is walking along such a city street, he will feel this characteristic atmosphere. He will notice, possibly to his surprise, that there is nothing particularly shocking or sinister about even the worst slum. There is, for instance, a considerable attempt to keep the streets clean. Rows of trees have been planted in some cases, and in progressive districts the borough councils have attempted all manner of improvements. Moreover, the people themselves are not apparently brutalized by the conditions under which they exist. They do not accost the well-dressed visitor, although his strangeness will be as obvious as though he had dropped from another planet. Still, he will have no grounds for alarm, no regrets that he did not leave his watch behind, no anxious glances in the hope of spotting a policeman. For the slum dwellers have taken on the character and the color of their slum: they are passive and gray.

Unmitigated dreariness; almost impenetrable gloom. Let the visitor, as he dismounts from his bus, look up at the sky. He may expect it suddenly to turn inky. He may think that night is upon him or, in a moment of panic, wonder if the sun has at last been extinguished. But if he lived in Bermondsey or Hoxton or Bethnal Green, he would know that this sudden darkening of the sky is a daily occurrence, as regular to London as the sirocco to the island of Capri. Sometimes it denotes the accumulation of smoke and soot in an atmosphere heavy with water vapor; sometimes it is a forewarning of rain; sometimes, simply a blacking out of the sky. But whatever the cause of this obfuscation, it oppresses the streets with an imponderable gloom. Houses, people, pavements become a shadowy part of the general grayness.

Day after day over the great cities of England the sky turns inky and leaks down gallons of sooty water. The rain trickles down every wall—and English slums are characterized by miles of blank walls—each drop burrowing its path through the film of grime. It cataracts from the roofs and dashes upon the pavement, streams into the gutters, and gurgles down the drains. There is nothing refreshing about this rain. It is simply water drops riding on particles of soot. The dismal trees seem to know that. They stand like wet dogs unable to shake themselves, bedraggled, utterly forlorn.

On the short, rainy days of the winter solstice the English streets are brooded over by an almost palpable atmosphere of oppression. The fog which creeps along the walls is palpable enough; so is the all-pervading dampness, a kind of yellow clamminess which leaves traces on glass like the mucus of a slug. The gas lamps in the streets glow like fuzzy balls, suspended mysteriously in mid-air. A heavy silence settles over the roof tops simultaneously with the blacking out of the sky. The city becomes subterranean, cavernlike. To be moving about in it is indescribably weird. It is like walking on the bottom of an underground lake—alone, except for half-seen shapes which might be men or monsters. One forgets utterly the light of the sun and of sunny things.

The English countryside manages to retain something of its shape and color even in the English rain. The wide fields and green woods are able to absorb it, and there is a sufficient expanse of open sky so that man

173

and beast and plant can see the rays of the sun stream-
ing down onto some distant field. Those strenuous
lovers of the countryside who insist on showing their
loyalty by striding across its territories, rain or shine,
are not to be balked by a shower or two. They don
mackintosh, pull on boots, place a hat on the head,
and march off down the slushy lanes, with that look of
conscientious satisfaction that the English wear when
they know they are doing the right, even if the uncomfortable, thing.

To talk about the weather, even though it is the most
satisfying, as well as the favorite, topic of English conversation, will not be particularly significant to those
who have a good idea of climatic changes, not only for
tomorrow, but for next July. Moreover, most foreigners
apparently feel they have said all there is to be said
about the English climate when they pronounce it wet;
but at the risk of sounding obtuse, an Englishman cannot dismiss the wind and rain so lightly just because
they are invariable factors of his country's climate. For
the keenness of the one and the dampness of the other
affect his very life, his character, and even his manner
of thinking. His industriousness, for instance, is largely
due to physical discomfort when he sits still in his
drafty and clammy house. His strong sense of duty
is an uncompromising dislike of ease and indolence,
which are impossible in a land without sun. His moodi-
ness, his contemplativeness, his predilection for abstractions are not so much manifestations of the divinely
discontented philosopher as symptoms of a man suffer-
ing from the effects of indigestion and rheumatism. The
obsession with truth which characterizes the English,

not only in their daily conduct, but in their metaphysical speculations, is not the search pursued by the Greeks of old and by the French today, but the melancholy disposition of people shut in by so many rainy afternoons.

We know that in the more ancient periods of the country's history the land was covered by forests. From the leaves dripped a constant moisture and the dark earth exuded chilly mists. Even then the English were, according to foreign observers, moody and ruminative, prone to a religion of the crepuscular variety, formalized in the cult of Druidism. The sunny gods of the Mediterranean and the East imported by the Roman Legions flourished only while an infusion of Latin blood and the Latin temperament enlivened the native melancholy of the Ancient Britons. When the Latins went, Mithras and the jovial gods went too, along with the arenas, the villas, the hot baths, and all the other amenities of civilization. Left to themselves, Britons relapsed into their old uncouthness, returned to their groves, crept back into their damp hovels. The Saxon invaders, in their turn, succumbed to the dripping climate and accepted a chilly existence on this earth and looked forward to a similar way of life in the hereafter. Odin displaced Jove; heathenism, paganism; mead, wine.

The history of the English, it might be said, has been determined largely by these three constant factors: rain on the English roof; beer in the English stomach; and heathenism on the English mind. Rain, beer, and heathenism; and perhaps one should add to the discomforts suet pudding as a fourth factor to be taken into account in an estimate of this remarkable people. These elements have determined the major English virtues and vices, their passion and their coldness, their work and their play. Some of their greatest achievements could have been produced only by an overdose of one or a concoction of all four. Their industry and their prosperity, their martial spirit and strong imperialism, their philosophy and ethics, all are characteristic of a people essentially nonpagan—nonpagan because of the absence of the sun, of the grape the sun ripens, and of the genial divinities, which the grape, in its turn, mellows.

As for the English, their God is a jealous God. Their religion is a harsh religion. Their law and government, their moral code and code of manners, are strict. It is significant for those who see today traces of the old Druidical religious fanaticism that the English adopted so wholeheartedly the God of the Old Testament, an exceptionally harsh and ruthless individual whom one can associate only with the colder and more rarified atmosphere. It is significant, too, that the English law has always been of the unhuman and relentless kind, based partly on the heathen theory of an eye for an eye and partly on the Hebrew plan of visiting the sins of the fathers on the children even unto the fourth generation.

The English like to think that their law today is just and humane. Over their courts stands the figure of Justice, a sword in one hand, a scale in the other. The function of the scale has changed since children were hanged for stealing; but that of the sword is the same— an eye for an eye, a tooth for a tooth. It is noteworthy in this respect how the English cling to the death penalty, even while admitting that homicide has decreased since the penalties of misdemeanors have been humanized. But even though they have recognized the validity of such incentives as hunger and poverty, and have modified the old hanging laws accordingly, they still do not recognize the more tortuous and subtle emotions which may likewise force a man to act unlawfully. Murder is murder, whether it is knocking an old woman on the head for the silver she has hoarded in her stocking or a clean, swift killing in a moment of unbearable emotional stress. It is as though the English take the attitude that one used to a rainy climate, brought up on a diet of ale and suet pudding, and imbued with awe for a Druidical god, could never entertain such tender or passionate scruples, could never be carried away by a sudden upsurging of desire. And this perhaps is true.

Watch the face of an English judge or the expressions of an English jury, those twelve men so good and true, sitting in judgment on a *crime passionel* or some obvious and tawdry murder whose motives and ramifications could only be explained by a psychoanalyst. Judge and jury alike are *obliged* to be impartial. They are expected to put aside all considerations of humanity. They must not concern themselves with the intricacies of motive and intention, only with objective evidence—with the blood-stained hammer (every English murder involves a blood-stained hammer, as though for the especial delectation of the penny papers), with the mangled limbs of the victim, with the relationship between the suspect and the dead man. As to *why* the crime was committed, as to the possibility that the murderer was in need of a doctor's rather than the hangman's treatment, these considerations are not only not examined, they are purposely omitted—for purposes of impartiality. But how can one be impartial in the face of human weakness unless cold with centuries of rain, stupid with gallons of beer, and callous with generations of self-flagellation for the gratification of a "jealous God"?

Rain, beer, heathenism—not omitting slabs of suet pudding, like the others gray in color, deadening in effect.

XV

National Sports

RECREATION in England, like education or accent or promotion in state services, such as the Church, is very definitely a matter of class. The common mistake of judging the whole people from the pastimes of one section of them is due to ignorance of this fact. Foreign critics are prone to draw overgeneralized conclusions from an attendance at an Eton and Harrow cricket match, from the Ascot races, or a county hunt. They assume that all Englishmen, for reasons known only to such a peculiar people, indulge in tedious games like cricket, breed beautiful race horses, and make repeated efforts to break their necks hunting a little animal like the fox.

In point of fact, neither cricket nor horse racing nor hunting is a representative national sport. These are the pastimes of only the upper classes. The English workman, for instance, would be incapable of hitting a ball with a cricket bat, even though he can elaborate over a pint of beer how Jack Hobbs, a national hero, ought to do it. He would not be able to tell a thorough-bred from a cab horse, even though he loses money every week betting on the former. Nor would he have any more idea than the proverbial American who is accredited with crying, "There she goes, the son of a bitch," when to call "Tally-ho" on sighting a fox, even though our English workman "kens" John Peel with his coat so gray for whistling purposes. All these games require breeding, money, and leisure, and the workman has not enough of these attributes to meet the English standards of sportsmanship. He is not high class enough to bat a certain kind of ball, mate a particular breed of horse, or kill a rare species of canine mammals.

It is true, of course, that the common man partakes in his own way. He follows the "England versus Australia" cricket matches with the compensatory fervor of the spectator; he studies the form of horses in the newspaper, special midday editions of which are issued for his exclusive information; he substitutes such blood sports as ferreting and cockfighting for hunting. Cockfighting, however, has been prohibited by English laws, notoriously lenient to all animals but the stag and the fox. And ferreting is not a city amusement.

About ten years ago the bastard hunting known as grayhound racing came to the rescue of the English proletariat. Grayhound racing was a perfect solution to the common man's needs for a blood sport. Tracks could be built in the heart of London, the races could be held on Saturday nights, the Cockney could own and train his own dog, and the Society for Prevention of Cruelty to Animals—to all animals except stags and foxes—could not object on the grounds of cruelty. The urban workman has made grayhound racing his own sport—and it has become a sport as exclusive to the lower class as hunting is to the upper.

For cricket the workers substitute football or "footer." The disadvantages of cricket are that it requires a smooth lawn, expensive equipment, and white clothes. No *decent* Englishman would ever consider playing cricket in anything but white, any more than he would consider riding along Rotten Row in a bathing costume. It is simply not done, and "not done" is more binding on these Islanders than the criminal code itself. Hence, a good Englishman would much rather go to prison for exceeding the speed limit than to be stared at for playing cricket in gray flannel trousers.

Although the lower classes cannot obtain the green, smooth grass necessary for a cricket pitch and can afford neither the elaborate equipment nor the special clothes for the game, they can always find an alley as a substitute for a football field, a couple of coats for goals. And even if they can't get a football, they can use any other round object, or make one with rag and string. It is not an uncommon sight in the London slums to see full-grown men playing this variety of "footer" on a side street; and every Sunday morning will see hordes of them on bicycles en route for the parks where, in deference to the full-sized field, the real goalposts, and the half-dozen spectators, they emerge in strange, striped shirts, short trousers, and heavy stockings, all of which garb, having been adapted from more formal garments, costs nothing to wear.

These, then, are the principal sports of the lowest class—or of those of them who are still active; and these pastimes are supplemented by certain more passive amusements. Drinking is the major of these. Not the old nineteenth century boozing which distressed the reformers and humanitarians to the extent of their inaugurating institutions such as free public libraries to combat inebriation; but a discreet, comradely type of imbibing, shoulder to shoulder at the "four ale" bar of a man's favorite pub. At the pub the workman finds all the comforts he lacks at home: a warm, smoky room, male company, a sawdust floor onto which he can spit, a genial young woman of immoderate bosom to handle the beer engines, an old chair by the fire, and a dart board.

All this can be seen at its best in a genuine London pub on a Saturday night or in any village inn on any night of the week. The foreign critic should recognize the immense significance of these institutions in English life. Let him not consider them as drinking dens or impersonal dispensers of intoxicating liquor. The drinking den and drunkenness are gone in England. Pub habitués are among the most sober elements of the population. They sit quietly in the barroom till closing time (10 P.M. in the South of London) and then, pleasantly stupified, stroll home to bed and sleep.

But let the observer distinguish between genuine and pseudo-pubs. If he makes his acquaintance with this venerable English institution in the West End of London, he is likely to be both misinformed and sadly disappointed. The West-end pubs are merely hybrids between American saloons and English night clubs, neither of which institutions is particularly attractive. Too many spirits and too few ales are dispensed. The places are frequented by too many smart individuals and too few sober ones, given a false glitter by the presence of cheap prostitutes, and not fundamentally warm, like the genuine pub, with the quiet satisfaction of masculine amiability. The foreign observer in search of the true London pub, then, must visit the specimens on the south rather than the north bank of the river. He might remember that all Olympic guzzling has taken place on the south—around the Globe Theatre, at the Mermaid Tavern, in company with Chaucer, with Marlowe, with Ben Johnson and Samuel Johnson, with Dickens—not to mention a host of jolly pirates who drank sitting over the Thames one day and were drowned in it the next.

With the discreet, with the genial, with the lovers as well as the observers of human nature, a choice London pub will be shared, only its name must be divulged as under trust. It is *The Yacht* at Greenwich. There are bigger pubs, older pubs, pubs larger and smaller, but none quite so characteristic as *The Yacht*. It overhangs the river at Greenwich, just north of the Naval College: set back in a little cove once used by the extinct fishermen of Greenwich, yet still retaining the appearance of a Cornish fishing village—at high water. When the ebb tide carries the greasy water of the Thames out to sea, an expanse of coal-black mud is uncovered. The boats in the cove lie helplessly in their cozy bed. Nothing moves on the waterway. The river with its stranded barges, its expanse of mud, gray waterside sheds, and derelict ships reverts to its primeval swampiness, upon which the late afternoon fog descends with awful melancholy. This is a time to see the river in order to appreciate the complete, the almost romantic, dreariness of London. The people in the street seem even grayer than usual. Even the red omnibuses have an ominous appearance as they loom out of, and disappear into, the fog. The scene is as sad as the mud flats at the mouth of the Thames. One is weighed down with an intolerable feeling of hopelessness.

At six, however, *The Yacht* opens its doors. This knowledge is something to brighten the forlorn dusk. Visit it first on a Saturday evening in summer, and walk through the low-ceilinged bar—the original oak beams have been slapped over with whitewash—into the room overhanging the river on stout supports which go down into the mud. Choose the hour of the flood tide. From the bar window, with a pint of ale on the shelf in front of you, you can see the London river come alive again. You can sense the blood pumped back into its heart. The stranded barges lift with the incoming water. The sailing barges hoist their red ochred sails. Tugs tear up the channel, heralding the approach of some big vessel for the Surrey Commercial Docks. Tramp steamers come one behind the other round Woolwich Bend—fish from Grimsby, coal from Newcastle, timber from Norway, grain from Russia, tin trays from Japan, passengers from Edinburgh and Montreal. Most cheering sight of all to the gathering occupants of the waterside bar are the paddle steamers returning from Margate and Southend, loaded with Cockneys on holiday, thumping up the river stern first, the *Royal Eagle*, *Golden Eagle*, *Crested Eagle*, and *Queen of Margate*. From their decks come the sounds of singing and the braying of the inevitable cornet. Everyone in the bar will have some friend on board.

In the meantime, if it is a Saturday night, this is an occasion for local talent to entertain the company at *The Yacht*. At first, the not too recent jazz songs are sung in ragged chorus. One remarks that the tubby old ladies sitting demurely along the benches join in only half-heartedly; but when the company grows tired of modern syncopation and reverts to the old songs—those grotesquely sentimental ballads about home, church, and lost chords, the old ladies come into action with piercing, nasal voices. This is what they have been waiting for, for these are the songs they know and feel about. Someone sits at the piano, rocking it with hefty chords, his beer swaying perilously on the edge and his cigarette burning another place on the ivory keys. "Down by the old *Bull and Bush*," they roar, with beery harmony and yearning expressions. "Daisy, Daisy, give me your answer true," "Little brown jug," "There's an old rustic mill"—everybody knows them. Everybody sings. Then there is a demand for individual talent, for solos. Mrs. Rollins, after a little persuasion, renders, "My fiddle is my swee' tart, an' I'm her only beau." A wag, one Joe Fisher, offers, "Eton boys, Eton boys, boys of the dear ole school." Miss Lizzie Hawkins obliges with, "Watchman, what of the night?" which is pronounced "luvly!" And so on, with droll and semi-improper recitations which cause loud and prolonged screams from those matrons with six children or more. Young 'Arry Mahoney is pronounced a "card"; Ernie Blight is told to "go on with you." Tears of laughter roll down flaccid cheeks, large bosoms heave up and down, hands beat the benches as three sedate old ladies suddenly break into "Knees up, Mother Brown," with action.

Suddenly the raucous voices of the barmen are hurled into the room. "Last drinks, please. Last drinks. 'Urry up, lidies and gents. Last drinks, please." It is closing time. The lights are summarily doused, screams rise on all sides—particularly from Gertie Summers, who has just been unexpectedly squeezed from behind in such a manner that she is compelled to shout, "Keep yer dirty 'ands orf, you." And so all drift out into the passageway. The night is clamorous with cries. "Goo' night, Ernie. Goo' night, Ethel. Goo' night, Liz. 'Night Jack." The lights in the waterside bar are put out.

As the stranger strolls along by the now dark and mysterious river, over which move secret lights, white, green, red, he may flatter himself that he has seen the heart of London. Now he can say that he knows fifteen million Englishmen, because he has seen fifty in the bar-room of *The Yacht*. What he sees in the lobby of his West-end hotel is of no importance compared to what he has witnessed on a summer night by the banks of the immutable Thames. For he has seen typical Englishmen not only of this year of grace, but of fifteen hundred other years, and perhaps of fifteen hundred to come.

2

The visitor to England who wishes to catch a flash of the old national spirit before it is snuffed out by the damper of the elementary-education system should visit a music hall of the more vulgar variety. There are few enough of them left in London, and these, like the most picturesque pubs, are mostly on the south side of the river. The prevalence of these lusty amusements on the south bank is not unhistorical. The City Fathers from pre-Elizabethan times have wished to keep their precincts sedate for the best purposes of trade; and as theaters were banned from the city limits under Good Queen Bess, so the more rip-roaring entertainments are driven over to the seedy districts on the south banks of the Thames. The audience on the north side arrive at the theater in evening dress and opera hats. On the south they arrive in caps, carrying their own bags of monkey nuts.

Let the searcher after English types, then, make his way to the old "South" in the London Road, close by the Elephant and Castle. If he is inquiring the way from one of the locals, he had better ask for the "Sarf." He will be directed to a decrepit theater, where he should ask of the peanut vendor, "Where's the gallery queue, myte?" He will be directed down a dark street, across a stable yard, and up to the gallery entrance. No doubt there will be a considerable line waiting for the nine o'clock performance. The visitor should wait on the end and, to allay suspicions, treat himself to a bag of monkey nuts, one penny. Then pulling his cap well down over his eyes, he can enjoy a close-up view of London's poorest and possibly most human inhabitants.

There will no doubt be a baby in the line, justly vociferous at being bounced about in the open at eight-thirty in the evening, when all respectable babies are in cradles fast asleep. The mother will insert a large piece of toffee into its mouth, which very effectively stops further noise. Or someone will offer a peanut, which likewise temporarily closes its gullet. Or a neighbor will seize the infant and proceed to blow bubbles from her own into the child's mouth. This procedure takes it so much by surprise that it is too bewildered to howl any more. Meantime, those mysterious and numerous cats which inhabit the London slums parade up and down the walls, conducting their amours with primeval gusto.

The conversation below consists of such expressions of opinion as, "Bloody cold night, ain't it, myte?" To which the correct reply would be along the lines, "Yus, myte. Ain't many people, is there?" After which one can proceed to discuss topics of current interest with the greatest of ease. The brash generalizations concerning English reserve certainly will not hold on occasions like this: one is lucky to escape with the history of one's neighbor, not omitting his family, his neighbor, and his neighbor's family, with large references to each of the children, their ailments, their visits to the hospital, their operations, and the like. The London poor have a great partiality for operations; and since their surgical terminology is as deficient as their imaginations are vivid, one has need of a strong stomach to withstand the stories of the scalpel.

At about a quarter to nine the first house comes out and the second begins to go in. One climbs several flights of rotting wooden stairs. In the gallery itself an overpowering smell of oranges strikes the newcomer in the face. Acrid tobacco smoke struggles upward toward the already festooned ceiling. The floor is carpeted with peanut shells. A gentleman clad in what looks like a cast-off Cossack army coat supervises the packing in of the gallery crowd. All hats, including the men's, are retained on the heads.

The satisfaction of the whole performance in these days of apathetic audiences who tolerate so much in the two-dimensional medium of the screen is the reaction of these galleryites to anything they disapprove. They have paid their fourpence and are determined to be amused. Those who have suffered in bitter silence from the nasal whines of emasculated singers and the seemingly perpetual motion of repetitious tap dancers, will be able to loosen their suppressions in the gallery of the "Sarf." Whines and clip-cloppings alike are met with a barrage of eructatory noises, blown juicily from a hundred or more lips. The next act is hurried on in consequence.

Female charms of the more voluptuous variety are met with a gratifying response from the "boys" in the gallery. "Yoo-hoo!" they cry; or merely twitter with pursed lips by way of the Cockney substitute for blowing kisses. The most appreciated jokes are those of Rabelaisian largeness. No effete subtleties here; but references to chamber pots, to the sexual processes, and the excretory functions. One should remark how the potbellied old ladies enjoy them, assuming one can hear above the running commentary carried on in spite of the hoarse abjurations of the gentleman in the Cossack coat, who is usually kept pretty busy trying to eject some offender, and being "chucked out" himself for his pains. Quiet is only maintained in deference to those frankly sentimental songs which smite a true Cockney with almost religious emotion—"Home, sweet home," "When you played the organ and I sang the rosaree," and the innumerable dirges about dear old mothers with silvery hair.

About eleven o'clock the gallery files out to the strains of "God Save the King" rattled off by a professionally patriotic orchestra. Out in the street, the visitor will need to gasp for air. He will feel like having a bath on arriving back at his hotel. But though he cleanses his lungs and his limbs, he should retain his impressions, remembering, perhaps, that he has seen an audience such as Shakespeare wrote his tragedies for, in contrast to the polite robots who feed in a fetid darkness on the pale emotions of Hollywood.

XVI

Country Life

ONE'S attitude toward the country in England will depend on whether one works there, lives there, or merely visits it. On first thought this may appear to hold true of the country anywhere else. But there is this difference: the English countryside is unique. By uniqueness we do not necessarily imply "the best in the world," although this would be the accepted interpretation among many Englishmen, particularly among those who have never seen the countryside of any other region. The uniqueness is due to the disproportion between the urban and the rural areas.

It is significant that one city, London, covers now a whole county, the county of Middlesex. Moreover, the contrast between city streets and country lanes in England is so fundamental that not only all resemblances to, but all possibilities of, nature seem to have been eliminated in the towns. England is now a wholly industrial country, the only such country in the world. It no longer makes any pretensions to feeding itself. A visit to the grocer's is a tour around the world. You have your choice of eggs from Denmark, Poland,

Egypt, and China. An English egg, like caviar, is a luxury. The country is, in brief, an appendage of the cities, like so many city parks or private farms, visited by the majority of people for relaxation or used for the production of choice vegetables.

In other lands, particularly in large ones such as the United States, the cities are still comparatively new enclosures built by man for communal protection. One can feel on their outskirts and even in their midst the silent, ominous loom of nature. The buildings, whether of wood or stone, have the appearance of being temporary structures, hurriedly erected to shut out the elements, the insects, and the beasts of prey. A reflective person still feels that his large and seemingly sturdy structures are small and fragile compared to the immense sweep of fields and the immovable wall of mountain ranges. He feels, too, that the busywork of the townsmen, their manufactures and commerce and stock exchanges, are still subordinate to the slow ploughing of the fields and the herding of animals. The townsman may be sharp-witted and sleek, but he is unstable, as it were, compared to the slow, heavy farmer. The latter has the final grasp on life. The farmer is the ultimate bulwark against the secretly hostile forces of nature. At all events, there have been ample proofs in some countries that the machine is weaker than the field, the stockbroker helpless without the husbandman. And for those who recognize the beneficial tyranny of nature this is a fortunate condition of mankind.

In England, however, nature has temporarily lost the battle. The countryside has long been at the mercy of the machine. It was small, green, and tender. In Roman times vast forests of venerable oaks had protected the fertile soil and the teeming, twittering life it nourished. Then an empire overseas was great enough to make a manor and a park out of an island, except for those remote extremities which were swept by Atlantic rains. Where there was nothing more than great, helpless trees and rounded hills, the process of denuding was easy. Trees could be cut down, grasses cropped, and a great park created, dignified by country homes, decorated by picturesque villages, in a seemingly perfect compromise between man and nature.

Then that ruthless and avaricious period of industrialism smashed across an open and helpless countryside, dumped upon it hideous factories, populated it with miles of dingy houses, swallowed fields and trees and villages down the maw of expanding metropolises. Within the memory of man the process has been carried to its bitter end. Little farms, narrow bridges, windmills, innocuous streams, village greens—we have seen them all wiped off the face of the country, and miles of brick go up in their place.

There is, of course, still an unspoiled countryside in England. There are still many places which retain the charm of rusticity. But notice the rusticity and the charm. The rusticity is not nature and the charm is not vital. These beauty spots are to be visited rather than lived in, admired conscientiously rather than felt intuitively. This self-conscious appreciation of the countryside is significant. It is a sure sign of the disappearance not only of nature, but of the country life. In those parts of the world where man lives in a proper subordination to the earth which sustains him, he has no conscious appreciation of green fields, dark forests, and distant mountain ranges. All his thoughts are unexpressed and dormant. The true countryman would no more think of visiting and admiring the country than he would think of admiring whatever deity he deems it politic to worship. One does not patronize one's patron.

The primary function of the English countryside, then, is that of a park land to be visited by city people. A minority of the population is found working the fields, and these retain some of the characteristics of their forefathers. Their lives are still limited, intense, and rounded in the pagan sense. They don't bother overmuch with the thousand titivations which science has had to invent to make urban life tolerable. They can still, that is, be contented and rested with small things. Sunshine, for instance, means something more inward to them than a coat of tan for showing off in night clubs. It means being warm, warm to the bone. It means the infiltration of vitality, as it means to all animals and plants. So, too, grass and crops mean something more than a gamble on the stock exchange on week days and a ramble across them on Sundays. They mean a living organism inextricably bound up with the organism of a man's own body. All the other rural sights and sounds have to the countryman their full, poetic significance—not self-consciously so, not as the copy for literature or rhetoric, but as the voices of living creatures, as important in the unity of life as the voices of human beings. And so the real countryman does not seek organized relaxation; he does not concern himself overmuch with the higher flights of the intellect; he does not write poetry; he does not talk overmuch.

There are a few such rustics left in England. Some authors—Thomas Hardy, A. E. Housman, W. H. Davies —have hastened to write their nearly finished history. The foreign observer who considers them part of the English people, as much a part as the Englishman who lends himself so fruitfully to analysis and caricature, may find them a long way from the cities, working their small farms, with one ear attuned to the earth which has supported them for generations and one to the encroaching whirring of the cities. If the observer can find village inns small and remote enough, he can study them in the comfortable confines of the taproom, listen to their shrewd small talk, examine their faces, ferret out their philosophy—in company with other sociologists who must now regard them as the last vestiges of a disappearing species.

To work in the country is one thing; to live in it, as a number of the wealthier English do, is another. These people now go to the country as they formerly went to the towns—for security and relaxation. For the English countryside is no longer formidable or lonely. It is still, however, quiet—not with that heavy silence which brooded over the groves of the Ancient Britons and made them sacred places, but quiet in the absence of the city roar.

These residents of the English country are really Englishmen in rustication—a distinctively national and, indeed, an insular type. They are the country gentlemen whose peculiarities have been so deeply impressed on the continent of Europe. In earlier times one of these squires, or milord as he became on once setting his foot on a foreign shore, snarled his way across Europe in a manner which brooked no thwarting. An occasional English nobleman visiting the continent on the traditional grand tour, impressed the "miserable foreigners" by the exquisiteness of his airs and graces. Lord Byron was such a one. The Europeans forgave him on the grounds of his beauty, but the gross squires they could never forgive or forget. They hated their big red faces, their loud voices, their enormous feet unfailingly shod in muddy top boots, and their manner of shoveling food into their mouths with alternate knife and fork. This squire type, however, this John Bull-John Peel monster is no longer characteristic of the English county. He has enlisted in the Indian army.

At the end of the eighteenth century a group of poets were young and poor and romantic enough to take a pantheistic view of the English countryside. They were by no means countrymen, though they preferred to live in the country, but they did see in tree and flower and field a source of inward pleasure and of lyrical expression. Their hearts leapt up, they tell us, when they beheld a rainbow in the sky. According to the textbooks of English literature, they were the first writers to view nature as an independent being. Before their time, nature had been interwoven with the life of man. Man was as much a part of nature as any other animal; only he was logically more important in his own estimation than a cow or a thrush or a dandelion. The romanticists shifted the emphasis. Cow, thrush, and dandelion were now the more important; man was simply an etherealized spectator singing their praises.

Although this was a literary movement, antedating the industrial revolution, it represented the compensatory attitude toward nature of all sensitive Englishmen who have been deprived of the solace of a country life. These Englishmen, poets, philosophers, naturalists, have so eagerly reached after this comfort that they have in the outpourings of their spirits idealized the English countryside into a veritable Arcadia. They have celebrated it in such mellifluous language that it has become rather exaggeratedly famous, like the Vale of Tempe. In proportion as the inexorable deprivations of industrialism strip the fields and woods, so do English poets concentrate on the remaining primroses and oaks. Nature has become a cult, where in wilder countries it is simply a background, not so much a source of inspiration and poetry as a means of livelihood. To the educated Englishman it is a haven to which he runs for solace and new vitality; hence, his passions for the downland and the woods and all those relics of rusticity which have survived the iron age.

Even the uneducated and unrefined evince this attitude in their relationship with nature. They periodically express the need of "getting out into the country," which explains the hordes of humble Englishmen which trains and bicycles carry from the cities every week end. These, however, have the attitude of visitors. They have neither the deep-seated respect of the farmer nor the passion of the poet. They swoop on the country with the frenzy of people needing fresh air and exercise. Fifty city youths and their girls will dash along on bicycles, more interested in keeping wheel to wheel than in observing the life in tree and hedgerow. Their appreciation of spring, for instance, will be limited to dragging up field flowers by the roots, lashing them on the backs of their bicycles, and scorching home as fast as they can go. The motorcyclist has a still more philistine attitude. To him the country means long, quiet roads along which he can attain fifty-five miles an hour without being summoned for infringing the speed limit. And to the middle-class motorist it means scooting along in a neat little box, with an occasional glance at a "good view."

Immediately after the war this irreverent sight-seeing attitude toward the country was so prevalent that it manifested itself in a development which was calculated to destroy the last vestiges of nature in England; for, in order to house and amuse the trippers, vast areas of the countryside were covered with all the shoddy appendages of tourism. The coast of England was covered for miles with bungaloid growths, which soon became large, hideous towns. The country near London was visited by mobs of Cockneys in motor coaches, who spread themselves over the downs apparently with the express purpose of littering the grass. All insects were trampled out of existence, except the flies. All birds fled in terror, except the most moth-eaten and shameless of sparrows. The whole countryside became a picnic ground. Fields were overrun, fences torn down, young trees uprooted. The last woods and copses were invaded by large and irreligious feet. It was like an organized murder of all quiet and little things.

This tendency has now been curbed or diverted. New ribbonlike roads route the holiday makers to other Londons by the sea, where a townsman can take a sniff of the ozone and pop for a "quick one" into a pub which reminds him of London. Cars, motor bicycles, and bicycles all tear in a whirling mass along these roads. Meanwhile the lanes, the downs, and the woods are forgotten again, except by those reverent visitors who, stick in hand and book in pocket, walk in pairs across the unoffended greenery.

The revival of walking—or, at least, the invention of walking—is symptomatic. It implies the return of haste-lessness, the need for a nearer communion with the earth, the awakening of a sense of respect. It is sympto-matic because it implies the need for a forgetting, of a shifting of the mind from the things of which bricks and stones and lights are the symbol to the gentle ob-jects which every blade of grass represents. It is the best that civilized men can do under the conditions they have evolved for themselves.

Whoever is a walker in England belongs to the com-pany who like their country green and merry. The others either contribute to, or are absorbed by, its soot.

XVII

Sex

A Note on Englishmen

I

ONE of the main tenets of English "good form"
—perhaps the first—is rigorously to suppress the
feelings, whatever the provocation. This atrophying of
the emotions is taught the English under the guise of
hiding expressions of fear, anger, hate, and the other
uglier human impulses. But apparently if one restrains
one emotion, one also restrains its converse; if fear is
hidden, so is the expression of enthusiasm. Banish
anger, and joy goes too. Suppress hate, and it is difficult to relax the facial muscles in the lines of affection.

In his earliest days at school the English boy is
taught by his fellows how to take a beating of the dis-
ciplinary rod without shedding tears, even without
flinching. The advantages of this stoicism are not apparent, unless it is to encourage the master to "flick
it on harder," as the English schoolboy would say.
Similarly, any expression of love, such as kissing one's
parents "coram publico" (more schoolboy cant) is

strictly taboo. Indeed, in an English public school, even to admit that one has a mother is bad form. It is not done. And the appearance of a sister, particularly an ugly one, sets the English schoolboy painfully ill at ease. If she is pretty and well-dressed, it is tolerable; but if she is plain and her hair is untidy, the youth feels eternally disgraced.

Under these circumstances schoolboys are able to make their fellows unhappy or ashamed of their parents for the rest of their lives. "Old Sanders's mother kisses him 'coram publico' " or "Old Nicholson's pater drops his aitches" or "Smith Junior's sister wears 'goggles' " will be the cruelest weapons one boy can turn against another. The result will be that Sanders resents his mother's attentions, Nicholson despises his father, and Smith avoids his sister.

In addition, women in the view of English schoolboys are sacrosanct, like God and the Holy Ghost. It is true that they need women, or the idea of women, for their formative sexual lives; but as far as their own feminine relations are concerned—mothers, sisters, other fellows' mothers and sisters—they maintain a profound feeling of reverence, not unlike the chivalrous feelings entertained by medieval knights—at least, in medieval literature.

Upon this groundwork of reverence is built a prurient knowledge of sex which is completely independent of any natural functions or of any conception of love. The sexual organs of both males and females appear to the young Englishman something to titivate or be titivated. An enormous curiosity begins to overshadow his puberty, a curiosity which is constantly frustrated by his inability to get any first-hand knowledge of what intrigues him or by his own uncouthness in attempting to do so. And so it happens that he becomes surlily convinced that most girls are congenitally indifferent to his needs and curiosities. All women tend to fall into two classes: those who don't want to, and those who want to so badly that they are fundamentally immoral. His early adventures and aspirations concern his attempt to fall in with one of the latter.

The average Englishman, if his outlook were to be determined by no influences other than those of formal education, might be expected to have the following sexual outlook: an unreasonable reverence for women in the abstract, an inordinate curiosity about them in the concrete, and a conviction that they are physiologically unsuited to him.

2

Madame Odette Keun, the French journalist, has remarked in her book *I Discover the English* the distressingly cynical attitude of the English toward sex. Though by her own account a middle-aged and ordinary woman (if she will pardon the lack of gallantry for the sake of argument), she was approached in London parks by complete strangers who proposed, immediately after passing the time of day, that she return to their rooms with them. Upon her indignantly refusing, she was met with, "Oh, come on! You like it, don't you?"

The Lothario who thus approached Madame Keun was one of those not common individuals who roam about parks making such bland proposals in broad daylight. He was not necessarily typical of the average Englishman, who, while he might well entertain such ideas, would nonetheless be restrained by good form from announcing them. However, certain aspects of the example are noteworthy: first, the latent attitude of the English toward women as falling into one of two classes and the assumption on the part of the adventurer that the French lady belonged to the group of those who "like it"; secondly, his conviction that this probability meant that a woman could work up the necessary enthusiasm as promptly as a man; and, thirdly, the ingrained English belief that a well-dressed woman who sat in a park by herself was there on the express purpose of indulging in casual fornication.

The first and second of these explanations have already been mentioned. The third is equally important, for Englishmen are not used to women who are well-dressed, and morality—partly inculcated into them by their own mothers—bids them beware or suspect a woman who is.

The most obvious and the speediest solution for such sex complications would appear to be marriage, especially as this ceremonial is not impeded by any considerations of *convenance*, as with the French. The notorious latitude with which the English and other Presbyterian nations regard matrimony should expediate matters. In practice, this is not the case. The young Englishman of the middle class cannot see his way to marrying until he can see the house he is to live in and the bank account he is to live by. The lower classes, with typical irresponsibility, are not so cautious. Early marriages are the rule with them. With the upper

classes, the opportunities for premarital promiscuity
ease the urgency of the problem. They marry at carefully timed occasions on the basis of what is known as
a good match. A few fall by the wayside along with a
particularly scheming chorus girl, but the certainty of
an early divorce lessens the annoyance of the disappointed parents. However, for the middle classes the
necessity of financial and social responsibility adds to
the difficulties of their own inhibitions. Consequently,
marriage is delayed.

An indication has been given elsewhere of what happens to the English girl in the process. She has had her
thwarted upbringing, she has been thoroughly indoc-
trinated with inhibitions, and she is, at the same time,
in a position of considerable helplessness, thanks to her
semiemancipation. All is very delightful in the first
stages of the courtship, provided she is considered by
the man's parents a good match. If she isn't, it is the
duty of her proposed parents-in-law for the good of
their son to make her as miserable as possible. If their
displeasure is full and hearty, she will not be allowed
inside the front door, which saves everybody considerable discomfort. If, however, acceptance of her relationship is not definitely withheld, but is merely
grudging, she may be sure of a frigid politeness in her
lover's home which will effectively make her feel herself a scheming and unprincipled hussy. Moreover, if
the young man is not in a position to support her—
"honorably," as the consensus of opinion would be—
the marriage is delayed indefinitely, during which time
she has the satisfaction of seeing her lover anguished
by his suppressed passion, yet too well brought up to

suggest a normal relief for it. She, as a partner to the situation, feels a complementary passion, but must refuse the consummation of it.

The result is that the Englishman is inclined to be a sorry lover and inapt husband. During his courtship he will blow hot and cold, to the complete bewilderment of his companion. Driven on by passion, he will advance rapidly one minute; then reining himself in, will retreat the next, as though to punish the girl for her presumed indifference. What he is doing is to punish both himself and her for the frustration of his own unspoken desire and the girl's unspoken refusal. A complex of sinister proportions is thus planted in the minds of both.

That the average Englishman, unable to break through the complexities of his sexual inhibitions, is not very successful in his more intimate marital relations, is possibly the explanation of the alleged frigidity of Englishwomen. No generalization could be more implausible than that constantly leveled against Englishwomen of their being congenitally undersexed, yet this is the common supposition—made in all good faith—of their husbands. The redoubtable Madame Keun who approached these problems with the intellectual honesty of the French appears to have made a good many inquiries on this matter. Sampling English husbands, she found in most cases an open or tacit admission that their wives—or, as they no doubt preferred to put it, Englishwomen in general—were unresponsive.

In all such cases the blame or misfortune should probably be shared by the man, and from him accredited to the inadequacy of his sexual education and attitude;

for besides the difficulties created by false chivalry and the grotesque curiosity resulting from inexperience, there is the puritanical doctrine of moral sin to contend with. Often no amount of reasoning or self-justification can overcome the sense of indignity or overindulgence which smites the "properly" reared individual in the act of intercourse. We have only to glance at the connotations of the act to realize this. The more prudish of the romanticists have contributed the largest share to this erotology: pink lampshades, champagne, exotic clothes, the *air mystérieux*, the sense of guilt, the unfaithful wife, and all the rest of it. The average Englishman—or any other individual for that matter—who approaches sexual intercourse with these elaborate notions of "love," is inevitably disillusioned by the matter-of-factness of what can never be physiologically other than a fairly prosaic affair. Any subtleties, like the necessary ardor itself, can only be in his own mind. They cannot be materialized for him, in spite of the sound advice of Horace and the other amorists. But the Englishman is preconditioned to romantic accompaniments. He is bent on them, so that if he lacks imagination and adroitness, he is doomed to a constant disappointment. Then he is embittered that a wife in the flesh does not change her shape and fancy with the lubricity of his own imaginings. Love, as Rupert Brooke has it, becomes a habit.

In countries such as America, where divorce is an easy solution, a constant changing of partners is the cynical translation into terms of life of the too facile imagination. In England the home which was worked for both preceding and following marriage outweighs the need of the flesh. The comparative stability of marriage is economic, not emotional.

These facts, these aspects of the Englishman's outlook on sex, should be taken into account in dealing with the man as a lover. Thanks to his initial chivalrous conceptions, the Englishman will have a good approach to women, the approach which will often make him exceptionally desirable as an admirer. He will be, in these vitally important early stages, a "gentleman." He will be gentle and considerate. He will understand when a woman is tired after an evening's pleasure, and not insist that she pep herself up with alcohol or nicotine in order that he may keep her longer out of bed. He will be able to leave her at her front door without reproaches or recriminations. In fact, to be invited in will mildly surprise, possibly even definitely shock, him. In England to be invited into a girl's house after 11 P.M. is tantamount to spending the rest of the night there; so that, if he is asked in, he may prove somewhat difficult to get out again.

So far, so good. But not even the Englishman can remain a gentleman under the impetus of emotions which make his very subservience to good form weaken what he calls his self-control. After months of a strange indecision, during which his companion may be uncertain as to whether he loves her or is as indifferent as the local octogenarian, he may make a sudden proposal under the obvious influence of some overpowering emotion. The strong, quiet, self-controlled gentleman is forthwith the prey of any shrewd girl. For although he may suggest, with all manner of brave arguments, that she become his mistress, it is quite obvious that have her he must, and at any cost.

If she wishes to be had at the price of matrimony, she can exact the forfeit after letting the man thrash himself into a state of self-vilification. He is a confirmed bachelor, he will tell himself, and possibly her. He cannot afford to marry. He dislikes the institution on principle. She is not good enough for him. (The opinion is stated, of course, the other way round.) And so on. The girl has nothing to do with all this save to look outwardly unhappy and inwardly to smile with a justifiable degree of complacency. For whereas the man is able to intellectualize his emotions, she can live hers with far more profitable results.

If the girl, once married, can continue to humanize the Englishman's other sexual notions with as much success as she has capitalized on his chivalry, the marriage should be a very successful one. The Englishwoman can generally manage to do this, but she is liable to be overwhelmed by the task which confronts her on the more arduous side of the altar. Chivalry is easy; aberrations and inhibitions are not. The Dulcinea role is quite acceptable; but no ordinary woman can become a Messalina overnight. Yet, if we say that the Englishman expects his Dulcinea to become a Messalina because he has publicized his intentions to the world by proposing marriage, we should not be misrepresenting his mentality on these matters.

The wifely role, then, calls for consummate skill, for endless patience, possibly for considerable good luck. It is in this regard that a foreknowledge of the Englishman's emotional make-up should be invaluable. He is congenitally no more excessively passionate than the Englishwoman is congenitally frigid. Indeed, it is likely that large quantities of suet pudding, deep potations of strong beer, overindustriousness, and a marked absence of sun, all tend to make him somewhat torpid below the neck. The woman's task would seem to be to adapt what is overemphasized within the skull to what is underestimated in the loins. The former needs to be toned down, the latter stepped up, and both humanized.

Small adjustments, which will come much more easily to the foreigner than to the Englishwoman, can be enlisted in this good cause. A personable appearance is the most obvious of them. Since the Englishman's romantic predilections require a sparkling eye, a coral lip, rosy cheeks, and the like, it is advisable for his companion to set to work with brush and pallet to present the portrait which will most please—assuming she thinks it is worth the trouble. Here, the American or the French or Japanese woman has an advantage over the Englishwoman. The latter is restricted or inhibited in her artistry. She must strike a cunning balance between the movie star and the Sunday School teacher, not so much to suit her lover, who would in the natural course of things be well content with the former, as for the benefit of her proposed relations-in-law. "Fast hussy" in England is a pretty serious accusation against a middle-class or respectable girl, and it will undoubtedly be leveled against her if she exceeds the traditional limit in the task of self-improvement.

For one thing, Englishwomen of the more sober groups (and this will be about two thirds of the female population) expect a uniform standard of dowdiness among themselves. While all are permitted to use a little powder, cheek rouge tends to be prohibited, and mascara is absolutely taboo. An American "hot mamma," for instance, would be instantly fallen upon by a group of respectable middle-class English women and mysteriously spirited away, on the grounds of unfair competition.

Nonetheless, when we remember those romantic expectations of the "well-brought-up" Englishman, we can see that the "hot mamma" would be the perfect answer to his demands in one respect. However, the success of the relationship would probably be precluded by those other chivalrous tendencies which the Englishman must express in order to be happy with a woman. Difficulties would arise when he insisted that she must be tired and she replied by recommending him "to snap out of it." Such a rejoinder from a woman would seriously disturb an Englishman's equilibrium, for he has not the training of the American Lothario in a land of torch singers, night-club queens, hostesses, and a miscellaneous assortment of ladies who arouse an emotion best described as "hot cha cha." An Englishman is completely incapable of addressing any woman—particularly a strange one—as "toots." Likewise he feels vaguely uncomfortable to be welcomed as "honey," while "big boy" justifiably fills him with a feeling of unreality. His chivalry, in brief, does not provide him with the necessary comeback. He is caught off his guard, and feels as helpless and unemotional as a fish on a marble slab.

The moral, we hope, is plain. Not only must the Englishman's eye be gratified, but his sensibilities must be respected. The American girl will find that her regular technique for entertaining a man will constantly interfere with an Englishman's poise. Even to put her arm through his on the street in the early stages of their acquaintanceship, let alone to clamp her cheek to his on a dance floor, will seriously complicate the relationship for him. He assumes that he is the one to draw her hand through his arm and to seek her cheek and lips at the proper moment for amorous expression, and he should be given time to materialize the desires he has no doubt experienced from the first into actions which do not conflict overmuch with his conscience. Otherwise, she may find him altogether too rambunctious, not necessarily because of his own inclinations, but sometimes from a misinterpretation of hers.

XVIII

Sex

A Note on Englishwomen

I

IN ENGLAND, as in all other countries except America and those ultra-civilized parts where women constitute the dominant sex, double standards of morality react severely to women's disadvantage. It is something of a distinction to be a bachelor; it is a social handicap to be an old maid. Kind-hearted observers are inclined to soften this discrimination by asserting that whereas men can please themselves in these matters, women cannot. A woman, they say, who is not good looking and who does not have the same opportunities (due, among other things, to the comparative scarcity of men), has very little choice in the business of selecting a mate. If she is not sought after and asked in marriage, she has to remain single, whether she likes it or not; and she usually does not.

Such a conciliatory attitude is humane but unrealistic. It is based too disproportionately on the hunter and hunted interpretation of sex. It is true that in a boy-girl relationship one of the parties is likely to be more urgent, the other less so, although motives and desires become pretty well disguised or confused in most cases. Still, as the French have it (and they are seldom wrong in these matters), "Il y a toujours un qui baise, et un qui se laisse baiser." But it is not therefore true that the male, suddenly feeling the rutting urge upon him, picks out the nearest female and tracks her down with the ruthless tactics of a panther on the trail of a gazelle. In other words, the hunting analogy is misleading: first, because it is confusing the urge of hunger with that of love; and, secondly, because it involves two different animals—the panther and the gazelle.

Nonetheless, Englishwomen are obsessed with the hunting metaphor, as are the women of no other nation. In more practical countries, where marriage is a social convenience and arranged accordingly, the parties concerned are not hunting each other by any stretch of the imagination. They might be regarded as a couple of pawns in a game of chess, if we must reduce plain facts to pretty figures of speech. Even in America, where the romantic conception of marriage has been inherited from the individualistic and aggressive puritanical tradition, the quasi-sexual emancipation of women has promoted them from being the prey of men to being their partners in the business of matrimony.

Not so with the English girl. She is quite convinced that she is, or should be, hunted. Hence her demureness, which hides an attitude toward sex amounting almost to apathy.

It is not particularly difficult to come at either the reasons or the symptoms of this attitude. The symptoms have been touched upon. The English girl is markedly demure, retiring, adaptable. She has little of the invigorating sexual aggressiveness of the French or the American girl, nor yet the subtlety of women without any rights at all, such as the Arabian or Indian woman. She is merely passive. Hence, she makes scarcely any effort to get her, or even *a*, man. Such tactics she considers highly undignified and, indeed, improper. No doubt women of other nationalities would call such overt methods equally reprehensible. They would be highly indignant to have the accusation of man hunting leveled against them. But their actions so belie their intentions that there is not the slightest doubt, apart from the accepted romantic reservations, that American, French, German, Italian, and Siamese women attract their preferred males with the same lack of moral compunction which distinguishes the courtship of other animals, except that the others are less impeded by various economic and social complications.

To put this in more concrete terms, we can reduce the difference between the English girl's tactics and the tactics of other women to a difference in the effort at attractiveness, in the use of the possibilities of self-exploitation. These possibilities, these aids toward charm, need no elaboration except insofar as they throw some light on the English girl's attitude toward sex. Her compunction in the matter of personal appearance has already been noted. "Men," Englishwomen are constantly telling each other with a fervor which belies their disbelief, "don't want a girl who paints herself." If you should ask why, you would discover that, behind the platitudes concerning the value of a good heart, a pretty complexion, a healthy constitution, and the like, there is a moral fear of cosmetics which enliven the face, of clothes which show off the figure, and of conduct which arouses a man's sexual interest. The immediate objection would be that "loose" women employ such devices. But this is still not the ultimate explanation. This can only go back to sexual repression and from that to the conviction that since all matters pertaining to sex, and particularly to sexual intercourse, are vaguely indecent, erotic tendencies should not be encouraged by look or word or deed. In proof, note the modern English connotation of the word *immorality: sexual irregularity.*

2

That many of these observations are true of American women, and possibly true of other women wherever the romantic conception of marriage is accepted, it is evident enough. The point is, however, that they are basically characteristic of the English. Moreover, whereas they only complicate the lives of those American girls who are brought up according to such standards—complicate them during such time as they are under observation—they *determine* the whole life of practically every middle-class Englishwoman. The extreme upper and lower classes, with their comparative absence of standards, escape. Sex for an upper-class English girl is a matter of cynicism and something of a bore; for the lower-class girl, an ordinary occurrence and something of a nuisance. The upper-class girl, with her opportunities for promiscuity, need have few repressions or inhibitions. Her troubles are more likely to arise from too much money, too much independence, and too much spare time—a pointless existence, with a few perversions acquired more from the dictates of fashion than from those of personality. The working-class girl, for her part, whether she is a city or a country dweller, is much too close to the phenomena of procreation, gestation, and the rest to develop a neurosis arising from repressed curiosity; and is that much happier in consequence.

But the repressions of the middle-class English girl, the neuroses which result, the sublimations with which she compensates her instincts are as prodiguous as they are secretive. To the religion-cum-cleanliness reared girl certain biological phenomena can only be loathsome. Thus she enters upon her puberty with a guilt complex.

In addition to this, most English middle-class mothers assure their daughters, by direct statement or implication, of the innate bestiality of men. Those pretty blushes which color the faces of English maids of sixteen or sixty in the presence of a man testify to a subconsciously outraged modesty. Yet modesty and bashfulness are considered definite virtues in English life; conversely, boldness—implying an *active* interest in sexual affairs on the part of the female—are among the worst offenses not punishable by law.

All of this is very important in a consideration of English womanhood in order that their peculiar position and behavior may be understood. It largely explains the extraordinary number of old maids. Many of these spinsters are single, not because of necessity, but because of their own sexual insufficiency. Yet most of them want to marry. A few prefer their independence, sometimes for professional reasons; but of the large numbers of middle-class girls who are condemned to an old maid's existence by far the majority resent the state without having the sexual vitality to remedy it. For in their efforts to be properly modest, they result in being colorless; while some, in their subconscious fear of love, will escape the obligations by ridiculing their admirers. When age creeps upon them, they are able to resign the cause, and can grow fair, fat, and forty in comfort.

This is not the place to apportion blame or censure. It is too characteristic of critics to simplify their criticism in order to belabor the object of it, instead of recognizing that they have a system to contend with which is indifferent to their thunderings. We have a system to consider. Thundering would be meaningless. The English girl, with her ignorance of sex, her distorted view of men, her passiveness, and her neglect of her appearance, is the product of that system. So far she is not to blame; yet we can only wonder if it would not be possible in her case, as in the case of many American girls whose parents and educators have taken the same trouble to pervert their outlook, to throw off some of the shackles of vicious romantic prejudice.

After all, the adroit use of cosmetics is not any longer an occasion for being turned out of the home, even in the most bigoted of families. A more frequent visit to a beauty parlor, a stronger partiality for baths, a preference for lighter and daintier underwear as against serge sacking, and, above all, a little more sexual aggressiveness (it can be called, for the sake of euphemy, independence) would give that so-needed élan to the English girl. Every woman has the potentialities for attractiveness; and the English girl, with her clear skin and resilient breasts, should exploit her potentialities too.

Instead, she sits at home by herself, and reads. How English girls read! Where the American or French or Italian girl is able to sit in a public conveyance and be amused by being admired, the English girl blinks at a book. She reads heavy books or romances by the volume, and reads them in public. Her guardians nod sagely and smugly to each other over this industry. The girl, they say, is so sensible, whereas Marjorie Tompkins is so flighty—going out to dances every night of the week. But the English girl is no more sensible than a horse who blows a trumpet in a circus. She is reading for necessity, not from desire. She is reading in lieu of being admired or made love to.

And so the foreign observer in England should note the habits of Englishwomen with a view to correlating them with their sexual attitudes. He should note how they go in clusters to dances, theaters, cinemas, and on vacations. Large numbers of them elect to live in barn-like institutions known as women's hostels, where all the restrictions usually associated with the juvenile inmates of a women's reformatory are applied with rigor to these presumably independent residents. He should note the general dowdiness of Englishwomen in universities and colleges and their self-conscious indifference to the men students, who are genuinely indifferent. He should note how their lives are centered around their homes and how few outside contacts they make as a result. He should note how many of them grow old first helping, then supporting, then nursing a parent. And this unjust bondage is sanctified and moralized and romanticized under the virtue of filial piety. The parents in return give nothing, save an air of faded respectability.

And finally he will note, if he has any intimate relationship with an English girl, how her conceptions of love are all cast in the mold of late nineteenth century romantic literature. A desirable man is not one so much of flesh and blood, not one who forces her kisses and fires her to return them, but a dream man who smoothes back her hair, places a cushion behind her head, and, with all proper delicacy, produces children from the air with the finesse of a conjurer extracting rabbits from a hat. And this man, like the conjurer, should preferably be clad in evening clothes when he springs the little surprise.

The other side of the picture is that English girls, in spite of their passivity and romanticism, are creatures of flesh and blood as well. Through their veins flows the urge of life. In their cells chromosomes are active. If they cannot muster up the will to live themselves, a man can do it for them—if he thinks it worth while. Let him pierce their apathy, give them the color they refuse to assume themselves. He has no need of illusion to mark the glow beneath their skin, the curves beneath their baggy "jumpers," and the straightness of their carefully concealed spines.

EPILOGUE

Western Passage

W E WHO have left England, perhaps forever, nonetheless feel ourselves always her children. Not that
we particularly want to; not that this vague affection for
the homeland is anything peculiar to the English. Indeed, every other national group within the hetero-
geneity which is the United States is more nationally
conscious than the English. They have their specific
and closed groups, specific because of alien traditions,
closed by an alien language. The English belong nowhere
—except to the very culture of America itself.

But it would seem that the various national groups,
while clinging to the pleasant aspects and memories of
their own country, have not so much the sense of belonging there as having lived a part of their life there.
They will regard this particular country as a place
which they knew in a former existence and to which it
might be amusing to return again. With the second
generation of these immigrants, the memories and
traditions tend to be less meaningful. Some slough off
the strange tongue which their parents use and which
they themselves used as children, with all the alacrity
of abandoning uncomfortable clothes. They want to be

221

Americans, these second generation Europeans, and to suppress utterly every trace of their foreign connections. It is significant how categorically they endorse the American way of life, how aggressively they adopt the most characteristic American standards. Then, American in all but name, they become fanatically antiforeign, heartily supporting those organizations and institutions and that legislation which would most effectively differentiate the American from any other (and hence inferior) nationality.

In contrast, the English in America have no need to segregate themselves when they first arrive and no desire to submerge their nationality in later generations. For in spite of their eccentricities, their alleged unhumanity, and their unpopularity, the English have prestige wherever they go. They are like good churchgoers: the object of everybody's scorn but comfortable to have around—honest bank clerks, industrious workmen, conscientious servants.

The strength of the English and of their culture is due, of course, to the very homeliness of their virtues. Their way of life, their mode of thinking, is the unimaginative way. They face all new conditions, as all new scenes, with the same prosaicism which underlies all their power and all their soundness as a nation and as individuals. Not that they are devoid of sentiment or the warmer emotions. As the nineteenth century emigrants sailed from the ports of London and Liverpool and Glasgow, they were dejected and miserable, straining their eyes to see the last of their homeland. The chronicles of the more humble of them tell of this unelaborated emotion. But once the land sank over the horizon, the homely virtues continued to determine their lives. We read how the English emigrant families conducted themselves with propriety and industry in the hold of the ship which was carrying them to an unknown continent. They met all hardships with patience, complaining only to their God, who has long served as a national whipping-horse.

In the year 1831 the Burlends emigrated from Barwick-in-Elmet, Yorkshire, to Philips Ferry, Illinois. John Burlend, his wife Rebecca, and their five children landed one evening from an Illinois River stern-wheeler, with a bed, some cooking utensils, and twenty pounds in cash—nothing else. In the manner of their countrymen, they fell on their knees and called upon God in a loud voice; then trekked into the interior. Twelve years later, they owned their three hundred and sixty acres of land, "at least twenty head of horned cattle, seven horses, including one or two foals, and pigs, sheep, and poultry unnumbered."[1] The good God, the Burlends were wont to say, vouchsafed these things to his servants. But they had the characteristically English modesty. They ascribed to a personal deity the labors of their own hands—with a view, perhaps, to obtaining some spiritual tax exemption at the final reckoning.

Thousands of Burlends and Smiths and Robinsons have been born and bred in the lush fields and gray cities of England, and brought their unpretentious virtues to distant places. Where other nationalities, such as the Spanish and French, have stormed or forced their way through forests and along rivers, the English have brought their beds, their cooking utensils, and their

[1] Their story, told by Rebecca Burlend, can be read in *A True Picture of Emigration*, in The Lakeside Classics, Donnelly, Chicago 1936.

twenty pounds, and stayed where they landed: at James-town, at Plymouth Rock, at Philips Ferry. In their hearts all of them were indignant or discontented with conditions in their own restricted homesteads. They had to go away. But once over the horizon, England was in-expressibly dear to them. They forgot the religious op-pression or the semiserfdom or the industrial hardships they had been unable to tolerate, and remembered only those sights and sounds which were not found in the new country. They spoke with profound nostalgia of the first cuckoo in spring, the smell of honeysuckle, the glimpse of a village spire seen through the heavy trees.

Even today, when England is no longer merry as it was in Elizabethan times, no longer powerful as it was in the eighteenth century, no longer imperialistic as it was in its Victorian heydey, these everyday objects continue to symbolize an indefinable charm, which fills the exiled Englishman with melancholy and longing. Governments and their legislation, politicians and their policies, people and their works induce the sense of hopelessness. The nation, it seems, is finished; it is no longer dynamic, no longer mighty. The penalties of re-spectability and security are being exacted from a people who have forgotten how to be adventurous. Their request of destiny is that the tides of human affairs should no longer run. The English are now hopeful where once they were self-assured. They no longer dic-tate to "lesser breeds without the law." They no longer loudly dictate even to their God. They are not now so certain that Britons never, never, never will be slaves. They merely will not be slaves—or, not if they can help it; and they don't help it.

England, we Burlends of 1937 assure ourselves, is passive, senescent. We must get away. There is no longer any hope in the gray streets of its cities or the watery meadows of its countryside. In any case, larger bombers than ours are to rip up streets and fields and people. No one knows why—unless it is to preserve an almost forgotten heritage, a heritage which we no longer cherish.

So we sail away on a large and comfortable boat to a large and comfortable country to live there largely and comfortably. The small and uncomfortable homes and hamlets of England go under the horizon. We are free. We can be happy again. We shall marry foreign wives who are prettier and more dashing than English girls; we shall live in better houses with more white and metal finishings than English homes; we shall breathe a clearer and drier air; we shall earn more money and live longer. But like the first colonists and all those later emigrants who lived largely and comfortably, we shall be filled with homesickness because we do not hear the cuckoo in spring or the nightingale on a summer's evening. As we drive over the long, clean roads, we shall miss a distant church spire and a gorse-covered hillside. These ageless sights and sounds will bind us eternally to England, making us envy in our hearts, perhaps, the unsecurely secure, the too respectable, the vainly smug, and the now hopeless people we were compelled to abandon.

Yet it is best to be three thousand miles away, in spite of the nostalgic longing for an occasional vision of chalk cliffs, hedged lanes, and quiet villages; and the memories of warm-hearted people who lived there. Visions and memories they must now irrevocably become.

Index